THE ROLE OF RELIGION
IN MODERN
EUROPEAN HISTORY

MAIN THEMES IN EUROPEAN HISTORY

Bruce Mazlish, General Editor

THE ROLE OF RELIGION
IN MODERN
EUROPEAN HISTORY

Edited by

SIDNEY A. BURRELL

Barnard College

THE MACMILLAN COMPANY, NEW YORK

COLLIER-MACMILLAN LIMITED, LONDON

First Printing

Library of Congress catalog card number: 64–16853

The Macmillan Company, New York
Collier-Macmillan Canada, Ltd., Toronto, Ontario

Printed in the United States of America

FOREWORD

History, we are frequently told, is a seamless web. However, by isolating and studying the strands that compose the tapestry of man's past, we are able to discern the pattern, or patterns, of which it is comprised. Such an effort does not preclude a grasp of the warp and woof, and the interplay of the strands; rather, it eventually demands and facilitates such a comprehension. It is with this in mind that the individual volumes of the MAIN THEMES series have been conceived.

The student will discover, for example, that the population changes discussed in one volume relate to the changes in technology traced in another volume; that both changes are affected by, and affect in turn, religious and intellectual developments; and that all of these changes and many more ramify into a complicated historical network through all the volumes. In following through this complex interrelationship of the parts, the student recreates for himself the unity of history.

Each volume achieves its purpose, and its appeal to a general audience, by presenting the best articles by experts in the field of history and allied disciplines. In a number of cases, the articles have been translated into English for the first time. The individual volume editor has linked these contributions into an integrated account of his theme, and supplied a selected bibliography by means of footnotes for the student who wishes to pursue the topic further. The introduction is an original treatment of the problems in the particular field. It provides continuity and background for the articles, points out gaps in the existing literature, offers new interpretations, and suggests further research.

The volumes in this series afford the student of history an unusual opportunity to explore subjects either not treated, or touched upon lightly in a survey text. Some examples are population—the dramatis personae of history; war—the way of waging peace by other means; the rise of technology and science in relation to society; the role of religious and cultural ideas and institutions; the continuous ebb and flow of exploration and colonialism; and the political and economic works contrived by modern man. Holding fast to these Ariadne threads, the student penetrates the fascinating labyrinth of history.

BRUCE MAZLISH
General Editor

CONTENTS

INTRODUCTION

If this selection of readings had been compiled two generations or more ago, its emphasis would have been very different. Then, undoubtedly, more attention would have been paid to interdenominational frictions between Catholics and Protestants, Jews and Christians, believers and nonbelievers. Some discussion of the struggle for religious freedom would have been absolutely necessary. So, too, would a consideration of the conflict between religion and science, which had lasted so long in the western world that some observers actually believed it to be inevitable and almost natural. In short, there would have been a marked tendency to emphasize changes, conflicts, differences: the Reformation, the religious wars and the struggle for toleration, the contest between secular freedom and the claims of orthodoxy.

These ancient struggles are not forgotten, of course. Nor have they lost their significance with the passage of time. To a large extent, however, they have lost some of the relevance they once had. Our own time has other concerns, and these have manifested themselves in subtle ways; for example, in the generally more moderate attitudes of religiously indifferent or even anti-religious thinkers toward religious belief. Whether this means, as some observers have suggested, that our generation is experiencing a kind of religious resurgence is perhaps debatable. It is true, however, that the furious crusades against religious orthodoxy conducted by nineteenth-century agnostics like Robert Ingersoll have a strange ring to modern ears, and one feels, almost uncomfortably, that blatant denunciations of religion are a bit like flogging a dead horse. Even the moderate and judiciously argued scholarly writings of someone like Andrew D. White, the first president of Cornell University, must seem to many a recapitulation of battles half-forgotten, of causes which, while they can still arouse antipathies, no longer seem so urgent as they once did. For those who turn through the pages of President White's famous *History of the Warfare of Science with Theology in Christendom* the tenor of his argument has an archaic, old-fashioned ring. And yet the issues that prompted President White to write the book were very real to his generation. Cornell University, when it was founded in 1868, seemed because of its avowed religious neutralism and openly secular outlook to threaten the bases of long-established belief. Indeed, it was in response to vehement criticism of the new university from a society still formally and overtly Christian in outlook that White sought to show how "interference with science in the supposed interest of religion, no matter how conscientious such interference may have been, has resulted in the direst evils both to religion and to science." Since 1895, when those words were published, both religion and science in the West have undergone a major sea change in their attitudes toward one another.

In scientific and scholarly circles there has, in fact, been a fairly clear shift in outlook toward religious belief in the twentieth century. This is not to suggest that many scientists do not still look upon religious orthodoxy as a potential menace to freedom of scientific inquiry. Nor, on the other hand, is every religious believer content to let the scientist go his own way in pursuit of discoveries that sometimes seem to contravene the truth of revelation. Nevertheless, I believe there are two major reasons why an uneasy peace between the two old antagonists has come into being since about 1900. First, the triumph of science in an age of increasing secularization has made it virtually impossible for the religiously orthodox or the scriptural literalists to force their views on the great majority of people who regard the findings of science as "good" in themselves. Science, for the mass of religiously indifferent human beings, has become a kind of surrogate religion with its own high priests, its own liturgical language, and its arcane lore far beyond the ken of ordinary laymen's language. Furthermore, the priests of modern science have been able to produce miracles in such profusion that arguments against freedom of scientific endeavor seem almost impious. In a world where human existence depends more and more upon scientific and technological skill it has become folly to attack those responsible for our continued well-being and, perhaps ultimately, for our very survival.

The second reason for a change in the relations between science and religion may be found in the growing consciousness among scientists that science as a method of inquiry is not intrinsically moral of and by itself. The techniques of science may be used for the most dreadful and destructive purposes. Scientific freedom does not guarantee that the discoveries of science will always work for the benefit of man. They may, indeed, be used to destroy him. Ultimately, therefore, the only assurance a scientist has that his work will not be used wrongly is the ancient moral code that sanctifies all human life. Of this fact many, although not all, scientists are acutely conscious. Moreover, their consciousness of the danger implicit in the divorce of science and morality is intensified by the threat that the secular totalitarian ideologies of the twentieth century may stifle scientific speculation far more effectively than old-fashioned religious orthodoxy ever could.

Since 1914 this sense of mutual tolerance has steadily increased in a number of areas Although developments within some fields of science, most notably physics and astronomy, have had something to do with this altered state of affairs, the impact of less subtle human experiences—total war, totalitarianism, genocide, and the threat of nuclear destruction—has probably been more significant. In part, the willingness of both scientists and secular-minded persons, in general, to see within the older religious traditions certain uses and values that had long been overlooked because of mutual hostility must be traced to the very success of secularism and religious indifference. Any body of beliefs is likely to be treated with greater tolerance when it is clear that such beliefs no longer constitute a menace to one's convictions. Religion, in this respect, has become a kind of museum piece, preserved and examined like the great gothic cathedrals, because it represents a noble, if seemingly outmoded, portion of the heritage of western man. This, let it be emphasized, is an attitude peculiar to the secular-minded or religiously indifferent, for there are still many devoted believers who do not regard the traditional faiths in this way. Never theless, the growth of a secular empathy for religion, particularly among intellectuals, has given rise, if not to a full-scale religious revival, at least to circumstances in which religious teachings may be recognized as having values to be found in no other area of human experience. In a world where little seems sure or firm it is just as well to accept the Christian or, more broadly, the Judeo-Christian tradition as any other.

This realization has been driven home by the knowledge, which is still not fully accepted by everyone, that the traditional standards and values of western civilization, which seemed so surely a part of the very order of nature, may not be so securely based after all. They cannot be deduced from human experience as one derives the laws of mathematics; nor do they seem to exist objectively outside the context of religious faith. While there are many people who cannot and do not accept this conclusion, there are unquestionably countless others raised in a secular environment who are willing to concede, albeit grudgingly, that it may possibly be true.

If this is a true description of our present state, the traditional values of the West that were taken for granted in an age when large numbers of persons adhered to the accepted orthodox systems of religious belief may need to be cherished more zealously in a world where they are not only unique but perhaps also dangerously vulnerable. Thus, suddenly, the secular-minded westerner and his fellows among the traditional religious believers have come to a rather surprising unity of outlook. In a world of totalitarian menace, in a world quite capable of destroying itself together with western civilization, the two old enemies with their sharply divergent viewpoints may have more in common than they ever realized before. The disappearance of freedom under a totalitarian system, it seems obvious, must cut down secular as well as religious liberty with deadly consequences to both.

A growing consciousness of outside danger to intellectual as well as religious freedom has had other effects of equal significance. For the first time in centuries the various religious communions of the West, including the followers of Judaism as well as Christianity, now see that they have much to defend in common. If secularism was, and to a degree still is, a threat to the existence of religious faith, how much more so is the militancy of a totalitarian ideological system which proclaims as an article of dogma the ultimate extinction of religion in all its sectarian forms? Thus we are witnessing in the middle of the twentieth century a groping for unity among the various religious bodies, a reaching out from group to group in an effort to find the common bonds of a western religious heritage. One consequence of this wide search for a unity of religious values may be seen in the ecumenical movement of the various Christian denominations and the increasing stress placed by religious thinkers not simply upon a Christian heritage but upon a common Judeo-Christian heritage in which, it is asserted, the whole of the western world shares to a greater or lesser degree.

For the historian this search for common values within the western heritage has also had significance. Once the history of Europe and the West was thought of in terms of change and conflict, but now the tendency of recent historiography outside the Soviet bloc is to emphasize continuity. The values of the West, it is increasingly felt, are based upon certain deeply rooted assumptions about the nature of man and the universe, the role of the individual, and the moral order in society. However deep the cleavages of the past, most westerners, whether they are Catholics, Jews, Protestants, or atheists, share and have shared for many centuries a common outlook about the world. Furthermore, this search for continuity has also led to inquiries concerning the uniqueness of western civilization. However much the matter may be argued, it cannot be denied that the West, for the past four or five hundred years, has developed qualities and attributes that have made it peculiarly successful, as no other civilization has been in the history of the human race. If nothing else, this civilization has become more nearly global in scope than any other. Since about 1500 it has pushed outward to every corner of the earth. It has developed a way of rationalized thought in the form of science and a set of techniques in the form of technology which ensured its virtual hegemony over large parts of the planet for a very long time. Indeed, its very success in expansion and domination has made it the most consciously emulated of all civilizations. This process of emulation and adaptation is one of the best proofs we have of the uniqueness of the western achievement, for it is being carried out in many instances by former colonial peoples who have frequently had a long-standing antipathy toward western ways. Despite how Asians or Africans feel toward the West, the fact remains that all, or nearly all, of them want the two characteristics of the West that seem to have given western civilization its greatest success in world expansion, namely, science and technology.

If contemporary experience is significant, however, this process of emulation and adaptation is not easy. Many underdeveloped societies are finding it extremely hard to undertake the first stages of the transformation that will initiate development along western lines. The experiences of this generation in that regard have further influenced the western historian's view of his past. Whereas once it seemed possible to believe that Europe and the West simply followed a pattern of automatic development which all other nations would follow in time, it now seems that there is nothing at all automatic about the creation of a scientific and technological civilization. The first steps toward creating such a civilization require painful, conscious effort and often a great deal of outside help and encouragement as well. One almost unconscious result of this striving has been a reexamination of the western past in an effort to determine precisely what sparked Europe and the European peoples to the kind of explosive expansion which has been characteristic of the West for more than five centuries. Moreover, the growing consciousness of the effort involved in creating this expansive movement has made historians very curious as to just what elements or peculiar combination of elements within the framework of western and European civilization brought this eventuality about. Speculation in this regard is not something newly undertaken by historians of the mid-twentieth century. It has been going on for a very long time, although our own generation has perhaps pondered the matter more deeply than preceding ones.

Increasingly, this speculation has led historians and other scholars to search more carefully for those unique characteristics which appear to distinguish the western civilization from all other civilizations. Although the element of chance may not be ruled out in any consideration of this kind, it must be admitted that even chance, in the end, may be explained in terms of a random conjunction of factors which may be subjected to historical analysis. Whatever one's predilections in this matter, whether the West was, in a sense, predetermined to this development or whether it came about as a kind of masterful stroke of fortune, it cannot be denied that in some way the West at a particular moment in its historical development was sparked by a singular concatenation of causes which made its history different from that of other civilizations. We need not enter into a discussion of value judgments in making this statement. There are still differences of opinion as to whether the rise of western science and technology was "good" or "bad" for the human race. In this instance we are only concerned with the fact that Europe, although it owed a great deal to the influences of non-European societies, suddenly found the means to utilize ideas and skills in a fashion previously unknown to the rest of humanity.

There have been many explanations of this phenomenon, and very probably we shall never have a complete and final answer to the many puzzling questions raised by speculation on the subject. We are not even sure that the various causes can ever be precisely isolated or exactly described. Historians have, however, come to the conclusion that among all the possible elements of uniqueness two probably played a significant role in the rise of the West. One of these was the Greek tradition of rationalism, which presupposed the existence of an underlying order of nature that could be described in terms of mathematics and understood by the human mind. The other is usually thought to be the peculiar nature of the western religious tradition. In this connection it has been suggested that the religious history of the West is not so much a story of conflict between material and spiritual points of view as it is a history of continuous compromise in which religion was somewhat less hostile to the emergence of philosophy and science than it has seemed to some observers. Although he was not the first to speculate on the subject, perhaps the most perceptive suggestion concerning this relationship was made by the great German sociologist, Max Weber (1864–1920), whose theories on the interconnection between religious belief and other forms of human activity, particularly in the sphere of economics, have been the subject of a great deal of debate during the past half century (see pp. 37–55). Weber was enormously interested in the peculiar pattern of western development which manifested itself not only in science and technology but also in that form of rationalized economic activity usually described as "capitalism." Weber felt that these manifestations of an underlying rationalism, while not entirely unknown in non-western societies, were so highly developed in the West that they might almost be thought of as peculiarly western. He believed their origins to be traceable to the distinctive way in which Christianity, almost from its beginnings, had looked upon and attempted to explain the connection between the human and the divine. His suggested explanation may be found in the introduction to a famous work translated into English under the title of *The Protestant Ethic and the Spirit of Capitalism* where he wrote:

A product of modern European civilization, studying any problem of universal history, is bound to ask himself to what combination of circumstances the fact should be attributed that in Western civilization, and in Western civilization only, cultural phenomena have appeared which (as we like to think) lie in a line of development having universal significance and value.

Only in the West does science exist at a stage of development which we recognize today as valid. Empirical knowledge, reflection on the problems of the cosmos and of life, philosophical and theological wisdom of the most profound sort, are not confined to it, though in the case of the last the full development of a systematic theology must be credited to Christianity under the influence of Hellenism, since there were only fragments in Islam and in a few Indian sects.[1]

Although many of the ramifications of Weber's thought on the relationship between religion and capitalism have been seriously questioned by a later generation of scholars, the above general conclusion is still acceptable. Despite its often intense otherworldliness Christianity, theologically at least, has a strong leaven of Greek rationalism, although it must be agreed that more than one leading Christian thinker has opposed the secular influences of Greek thought on the

[1] Max Weber, *The Protestant Ethic and the Spirit of Capitalism*, trans. Talcott Parsons (New York: 1930) p. 13.

grounds that divine truth is beyond human comprehension. Christianity, however, could not overcome the influences of the Greco-Roman environment in which it originally expanded into a universal faith. Many of its earliest leaders were men of great intellectual capacity who also had a wide knowledge of antique literature and philosophy. Saul of Tarsus (known afterwards to Christians as St. Paul) was a perfect synthesis of Hebraic, Christian, and Greek influences. St. Augustine, the greatest of the Latin fathers of the early Church, made use of the intellectual skills of a Hellenized education even when he seemed to reject them. What was very probably most significant about Christianity was the fact that over the centuries, even when it seemed to have lost touch with its ancient rationalist influences, it continued to develop a very sophisticated way of explaining the natural and the divine which, as Weber noticed, had no counterpart in any other great religion. Thus Christianity, for all of its bitter opposition to secular philosophy and later to natural science, had within itself a mode of thinking particularly congenial to both. Men trained in this mode of thought could not resist the enticements of philosophy, mathematics, or natural science. It is not surprising, therefore, that in every great intellectual crisis of western history, where ecclesiastical authority sought to suppress some aspect of secular learning because it seemed dangerous to revealed truth, secular learning ultimately triumphed. The Christian thinkers of the Latin West, almost in spite of themselves, could not let secular knowledge alone. They had to find a means of absorbing it into the body of Christian thought. Nor could they believe that there was any contradiction between the truths of the natural world and the truths of God, since this would deny the essential perfection and the ultimate rationality of divine creation. God could not contradict Himself; nor was He irrational. The outstanding example of the triumph of this assumption may be seen in the work of the great medieval scholastic philosopher, St. Thomas Aquinas, who, in the face of ecclesiastical prohibitions, successfully undertook to incorporate the secular writings of Aristotle into the thought of medieval Christianity. Although Aristotle's works proved a hindrance to the development of scientific thought at a later date, the existence of such a large body of natural philosophy within the framework of Christian theology stood as a kind of permanent temptation to those who wished to speculate further about the order of nature. Thus, by a kind of paradox, medieval Christianity, which has often been regarded as repressive and deluded in its attitude toward science and philosophy, has more recently come to be thought of as the link between the

Greek rationalist tradition and the modern world. The late Alfred North Whitehead, one of the leading philosophers of modern science, was so convinced of the importance of the medieval contribution to the later development of science that he felt there could have been no great "scientific revolution" in the seventeenth and eighteenth centuries if the Christian middle ages had not been so preeminently rational and Aristotelian in outlook. If medieval men had not believed as firmly as the Greeks in the existence of general principles that gave order to the universe, if they had not believed, in Whitehead's words, that every event "may be correlated with its antecedents in a perfectly definite manner," later scientific speculation would have been inconceivable.

In this context the history of religion in the West looms much larger than it did in academic studies a generation or two ago. The sharp divergences, the periodic, almost revolutionary, breaks between historic eras that most historians used to see as part of the essential pattern of western history have now been subsumed under a broader pattern of continuity resulting from our increased awareness of a common history which, despite gaps, and despite twists and turns, reaches back to the world of classical antiquity. Christianity in the Latin West, during the first fifteen hundred years of its existence, provided a bridge from the Greco-Roman world to our own. Its importance to western civilization did not cease with that formidable contribution. In spite of its sometimes repressive influences, it contained within itself not only a tradition of rationalism but also a sense of morality, an ethical direction, which, although often imperfectly realized, implanted in western thought a set of moral assumptions that have guided much of western political and social development.

THE CHURCH IN A CHANGING WORLD:
A CONTRIBUTION TO THE
INTERPRETATION OF THE RENAISSANCE *

Wallace K. Ferguson

One of the major creations of the medieval world was the massive, supranational institution of the western Latin Church, whose supreme pontiffs at the height of their power during the thirteenth century laid claim to the suzerainty of all Christendom. For centuries its existence was taken for granted, and the Church was praised or criticized according to one's point of view. More recently, however, scholars of very divergent outlooks have come to regard the medieval Church quite differently, namely, as one of the most unique, even extraordinary, achivements of western man. Whatever one's judgment about the Church, it cannot be denied that under medieval conditions the organization of such a strong and effective system of international ecclesiastical administration was one of the important facts of western history. Furthermore, despite the later diminution of its authority, the continued existence of this powerful organization affected the history of the West as have few other influences. The transition of the medieval Church from the pinnacle of thirteenth-century greatness to the nadir of weakness on the eve of the Reformation therefore marks one of the most significant changes in the history of Europe and the West. Whether this period was one of Renaissance or "rebirth," as has sometimes been argued, or merely one in which certain intellectual and social emphases shifted slowly from a medieval to a modern point of view has long been discussed by historians. In the selection below Professor Wallace K. Ferguson, who has devoted an active scholarly career to the study of this period, describes both the changes in the nature of the late medieval Church and the problem of the Renaissance in historical thinking.

The historical interpretation of that phase in the development of European civilization represented by the fourteenth, fifteenth, and

* Reprinted with the permission of the author and the editors of the *American Historical Review* (**LIX,** 1953, 1–18, with omissions).

sixteenth centuries poses a problem that has aroused much interest and no little controversy among scholars in the ninety-odd years since Burckhardt first treated these centuries as a period in the history of Italian civilization and labeled it the Renaissance. Since then, scholars who did not share Burckhardt's preconceptions, or who were interested primarily in other countries or in some particular aspect of culture, have presented widely divergent views of the spirit, content, and chronological limits of the Renaissance, with the result that the value of the concept for purposes of periodization has been greatly vitiated. Much of the confusion concerning the Renaissance arises, I think, from the fact that it has been used indiscriminately as a style concept or to denote an intellectual movement, and that, when considered as a historical period, it has commonly been regarded from the point of view of one country or one particular cultural or religious interest, so that its interpretation has been constructed upon too narrow a foundation. It seems to me that, if we consider the economic, social, and political, as well as the intellectual, aesthetic, and religious life of the centuries from 1300 to 1600, we shall find a certain unity of development in all the countries of western Europe. It seems to me, too, that, if the various aspects of their civilization are related to one another in a reasonably well coordinated synthesis, these three centuries may be treated as a period in the history of western European civilization as a whole, and that such a periodic concept may have sufficient validity to serve as a useful, if not indispensable, instrument of historical thought. For this period the term Renaissance may not be well chosen, but it is still the only commonly accepted term we have for a crucially important historical period, and one that cannot be treated satisfactorily by the simple device of attaching it to either the medieval or the modern age, or by dividing it between them.

It is, indeed, the distinguishing characteristic of these centuries that they are neither medieval nor modern, but represent a transitional stage which has a character of its own. In a paper read at the meeting of the Modern Language Association,[1] I defined the Renaissance as a period characterized by the gradual shift from one fairly well coordinated and clearly defined type of civilization to another, yet at the same time possessing in its own right certain distinctive traits and a high degree of cultural vitality. As a more precise hypothesis I suggested that it was a transition from a civilization that was predominantly feudal and ecclesiastical in its social, political, and cultural manifesta-

[1] W. K. Ferguson, "The Interpretation of the Renaissance: Suggestions for a Synthesis," *Journal of the History of Ideas*, XII (1951), 483–95.

tions and agrarian in its economic foundations, to one that was predominantly national, urban, secular, and laic, in which the economic center of gravity had shifted from agriculture to commerce and industry and in which a simple money economy had evolved into capitalism. What I want to consider here is the problem of the Church and the papacy in this synthesis. To what extent do they fit? And to what extent does this approach to the interpretation of the Renaissance serve to illuminate a crucial segment in the history of the Church?

The origins of the Church, of course, carry us back to a period before the Middle Ages. From that early period it inherited not only its basic doctrine but also the concept of universality and the hierarchical organization that have remained constant throughout its history. In considering what was peculiarly medieval in the Church, however, and therefore likely to change with the passing of medieval civilization, we need go no further back than the centuries in which feudalism was taking shape, that is, roughly the eighth, ninth, and tenth centuries. In these centuries, if we accept Pirenne's thesis, western Europe had been reduced to an almost purely agricultural economy. And I think we might describe feudalism as fundamentally the adaptation of social and political organization to an economy in which land was almost the only form of wealth. Under these circumstances, central governments lacked the financial resources to govern effectively, so that legal jurisdiction and governmental authority were parceled out among the great landholders. Under these circumstances, too, the clergy, as one of the two classes that did not work the land yet had a very important function to perform, became a landholding class. Even earlier, in the Merovingian period, bishops had become administrative officers with secular rule over their cities. Now, as feudal lords, the bishops and abbots became the rulers of fiefs, barons ecclesiastical with sovereign rights in their baronies. From this period on, the Church was committed to the exercise of temporal authority and to great possessions. But, by the nature of feudal tenure, a lord was also a vassal. And the barons ecclesiastical were at the same time vassals of secular lords: kings or emperors. From this arose much interference by laymen in the election of church officials, and the ill-omened figure of Simon Magus cast its shadow across the Church. This was the period in which the Church was most completely feudalized. In their dual capacity as feudal vassals and church officers, prelates were forced to divide their services, often somewhat unequally, between God and Mammon, but they also exercised a great deal of independent authority. The utter inadequacy of fiscal income made effective central government almost impossible for either the papacy or the monarchies, so that the conflict of secular and spiritual interests operated on the level of diocese and fief rather than of Church and state in the broader sense.

The eleventh century marked the beginning of a tremendous revival in every branch of medieval civilization. Regular commercial relations were re-established between Italy and the Levant. From the seacoasts trade spread inland until the whole of western Europe was covered with a network of trade routes along which traveled not only merchants but also pilgrims, crusaders, students, and churchmen on official business. At intervals along these trade routes old cities revived or new ones sprang up. They became centers of local trade and skilled industry and, at the same time, furnished a market for surplus agricultural products. The twelfth and thirteenth centuries were characterized by a steadily growing prosperity in both country and city. The population of western Europe probably doubled during this period. Money economy, reintroduced through commerce and industry in the cities, spread to the countryside and made possible the partial conversion of landed wealth into fluid wealth that could be mobilized and concentrated. But, though this economic revival received its initial impetus from trade and depended for its continuing growth on the growth of cities, European society still retained in main outlines the structure which had been given it by the feudal system and the Church. The vigorous culture which made the twelfth and thirteenth centuries the classic period of medieval civilization was pre-eminently the culture of the feudal nobility and the clergy.

Feudalism, indeed, lasted long after the passing of that condition of almost exclusive agricultural economy in which it had been formed and which had justified its existence. The rights and privileges of the dominant feudal classes were protected by their monopoly of military force, by long-established jurisdictional authority, and by custom so ingrained that no other form of social and political organization could be imagined. As Joseph Calmette has observed, feudalism had become a kind of Kantian category, in terms of which the medieval mind perceived the social world.[2] Nevertheless, the growth of a money economy made possible, even in this period, the gradual recovery by central governments of some of the powers that had been lost in practice, if not in theory, during the early feudal era. In the early stages of this development, however, the government of the Church was in a position to take advantage of the new situation to better effect than were the feudal monarchies. Though partially feudalized in

[2] Joseph Calmette, *Le Monde féodal* (Paris, 1946), p. 169.

practice, the Church had never been as feudalized in theory as were the secular states. Its hierarchical principle was deeply rooted in both tradition and dogma. The feudal system, it is true, was also in theory hierarchical; but the feudal hierarchy consisted of a fortuitous network of personal relations which changed its form with each generation and which the accidents of marriage and inheritance rendered increasingly chaotic. The hierarchy of the Church, on the other hand, was a rationally organized administrative system, modeled upon that of the Roman Empire. Whereas the secular monarchies could establish effective state government only by destoying the feudal hierarchy as a political reality, the ecclesiastical monarchy had only to tighten its control of the hierarchy to make it an effective instrument of central government.

Even so, this was no easy task, for the officers of the Church were also vassals of emperors or kings. Bishops resisted the extension of papal authority not only because it infringed upon their independent diocesan jurisdiction but also because, in many cases, they felt a prior loyalty to the king or emperor who had nominated and enfeoffed them. This was the most serious obstacle to the growth of a strong centralized government in the Church. The vigorous assertion of the papal monarchy by Gregory VII led inevitably to the Investiture Controversy with the emperors and to less overt conflicts with other kings and princes. It also led to an unprecedented expansion of the claims of papal supremacy from the ecclesiastical into the temporal sphere. For, so long as the officers of the Church were also temporal lords, whose support was essential to secular rulers, the government of the Church could not be disassociated from that of the state. An effective papal monarchy within the Church could, therefore, be achieved only by establishing papal supremacy over the secular states. In this the popes were never entirely successful, but in the age of Innocent III they came very close to the fulfillment of their ambition. In their contest with the powers of this world the popes could count on the immense spiritual authority conferred upon them by unchallenged faith in the saving power of the Church. Their spiritual weapons were not yet blunted by overuse. They enjoyed the prestige of leading the military might of Christendom against the infidel; and they were actively supported by all the reforming elements in the monastic orders, by the doctors of the new scholastic learning, and by the development of canon law in the new universities. It must not be forgotten that the assertion of papal supremacy began as a reform movement at a time when reform of the Church was sadly needed. There is something, too, in Heinrich von Eicken's theory that the supremacy of the Church over temporal governments was the logical extension into practice of the ascetic conviction of the worthlessness of all things worldly.[3] At any rate, the concern with temporal affairs, which threatened eventually to secularize the Church, had in the twelfth century the full support of St. Bernard and all the most ascetic elements in both the secular and regular clergy.

Despite all these advantages, it is doubtful whether the papacy or the Church as an institution could have achieved the dominant position they held in the age of Innocent III if political and social life had not still been cast in the feudal mold—and that not only because secular governments were still too much weakened by feudal particularism to resist the encroachments of the spiritual authority upon the temporal sphere. The privileged legal status of the clergy fitted naturally into a society in which all legal status depended upon social status. The immunity of the clergy from secular jurisdiction was only one of many immunities, akin to that of the burghers or any other corporate body. The ecclesiastical courts and the canon law competed not with state courts and state law but with a bewildering variety of feudal and urban courts and laws. Everywhere the Church had the advantage that its institutions were universal, while those of the secular world were local and particular. The universality of the Church, indeed, found its perfect complement in the particularism and localism of feudal society. There could be little real conflict between a knight's loyalty to his immediate lord and the Christian's loyalty to the head of the *Respublica Christiana* [Christian Commonwealth or Christendom]. Seldom did these centuries witness any type of warfare between the extremes of the localized feudal brawl and the crusade against the infidel. Finally, it was largely due to the conditions of life in a feudal society that the clergy were able to maintain a practical monopoly of education. As the only class in society which had a felt need for these things, the clergy became the principal protagonists of learning, music, and art. They were thus able to give them a direction consonant with their own interests, and to place upon them the stamp of a universal uniformity that did much to impede the growth of national sentiment or national cultures. The feudal nobility had their vernacular literatures —troubadour lyric, chanson, romance, or Minnesang—but serious thought served the Church. The best brains of Europe functioned below a tonsure. And what medieval men had of visual beauty or the concourse of sweet sounds they owed to the universal Church.

[3] Heinrich von Eicken, *Geschichte und System der mittelalterlichen Weltanschaung* (Stuttgart, 1923), pp. 325 ff.

The conditions so uniquely favorable to papal supremacy and to the dominant position of the Church in European society lasted until about the end of the thirteenth century. Even before that time, however, there were signs, though the cloud was no larger than a man's hand, that the halcyon days were passing. The conflict between the thirteenth-century popes and the viper brood of the Hohenstaufen ended in the practical destruction of the Empire. But, in the process, the papacy lost something of the moral prestige that had been its greatest asset in the days of the Investiture Controversy. A moral conflict had degenerated into a squabble over territorial sovereignty in Italy. The spiritual weapons of the Apostolic See had been used too freely in defense of the material patrimony of St. Peter, and popes had too often cried crusade when there was no crusade. So far as any contemporary could observe, however, the papacy was stronger than ever. The Empire was shattered, and, during the greater part of the thirteenth century, France was ruled by a saint and England by a pious fool, neither of whom would offer effective resistance to the spiritual ruler of Christendom. When in 1300 Boniface VIII proclaimed the first Jubilee Year, it seemed as though all Europe had come to Rome to pour its varied coinage into the papal coffers. Two years later, in the bull *Unam Sanctam*, Boniface proclaimed in uncompromising terms the subjection of the temporal to the spiritual authority and concluded by declaring that, for all human creatures, obedience to the Roman pontiff is altogether necessary to salvation. The storm that broke immediately thereafter indicated the extent to which conditions had changed. Philip the Fair was no saint, and Edward I no pious fool. Nor were these sovereigns content to act as mere feudal suzerains within their kingdoms. The reigns of these two kings mark the first decisive stage in the transition from feudal to national monarchy, and a national monarch, determined to be master in his own state, could scarcely tolerate either the papal claims to supremacy or the immunity of the clergy from royal jurisdiction and royal taxation. In the rising national monarchies the papacy met for the first time a secular power too strong for it. The arrest of the aged pope at Anagni marked the end of a period which had opened with an emperor standing barefoot in the snow before the gates of Canossa.

The crisis precipitated by the conflict between Boniface VIII and Philip the Fair led to a series of events which seriously undermined the authority and prestige of the papacy; the long exile at Avignon under the shadow of the French monarchy, the scandal of the Great Schism, the conciliar movement, and the anarchy in the Papal States. All of these events aggravated the difficulties inherent in the position of the Church in a changing world. Yet their significance may easily be exaggerated. The anarchy in the Papal States which made Rome unsafe was not new. There had been schisms before the Great Schism, and antipopes before Clement VII. As Guillaume Mollat has recently pointed out, the absence of the popes from Rome was not unprecedented nor necessarily disastrous.[4] It has been calculated, indeed, that "between the years 1100 and 1304, that is, two hundred and four years, the popes lived one hundred and twenty-two outside Rome and eighty-two in Rome: a difference of forty years in favor of absence." [5]

What seems to me more significant than these external events in the history of the papacy is the profound though gradual change which took place in the whole civilization of western Europe in the three centuries following 1300. It was a change caused by the interaction of political and social factors, complicated by shifts in the social balance and by the imponderable element of a changing *Weltanschauung* [world outlook]. But one factor at least was, I think, of basic importance: the expansion within feudal society of a money economy during the preceding two or three hundred years. By the end of the thirteenth century it had begun to disintegrate a system never intended for it. Even before that time, the manorial system, with its exchange of labor and produce for the use of land and its closely integrated relation of landholders to dependent workers, had begun to be replaced by a system of cash payments—of rents, leases, and wages. The result was a fundamental change in the economic and social foundations of feudalism. The disrupting effect of this change was aggravated by widespread famines in the early years of the fourteenth century, by the depopulation of Europe resulting from the Black Death and the succession of only relatively less fatal epidemics that followed, by the devastation of France during the Hundred Years' War, by the cessation of colonization and of the assarting of waste land, in short by a series of economic crises and depressions which bred intense social unrest and seriously undermined the economic stability of the feudal classes, including the landholding clergy, and loosened their hold upon the land and its people.

At the same time that the economic and social foundations of feudalism were crumbling, the political and jurisdictional powers of the feudal nobles were being absorbed by the central governments in the great national states and in the smaller principalities of Germany

[4] Guillaume Mollat, *Les Papes d'Avignon* (Paris, 1949), pp. 9 ff.
[5] Louis Gayet, *Le Grand Schisme d'Occident* (Florence, 1889), p. 3.

and the Netherlands, as they had been already in the city-states of Italy. The money economy which undermined the independence of the feudal classes served to increase the powers of central government. Money furnished the sinews of administration as of war, and though the total wealth of the European states may not have increased materially during the period of economic crisis from 1300 to about 1450, governments everywhere were learning to utilize the available wealth to better effect by levying new taxes, by imposing import, export, and excise duties, by borrowing from the great Italian banking houses, and, in general, by evolving a more efficient fiscal system. The change in military technique from the feudal array to the royal armies and mercenary companies of the Hundred Years' War is but one symptom of a process which, by the end of the fifteenth century, had subordinated feudal particularism to royal absolutism and had transformed the feudal vassal of the Middle Ages into the courtier of the early modern period.

Meanwhile, in the urban centers of commerce and industry an equally fundamental change was taking place. Even before 1300, in Italy and the Netherlands, a simple money economy had begun to develop into an embryonic capitalist system. That development continued steadily during the following centuries and spread to all parts of western Europe. The first hundred and fifty years or so of this period, it is true, lacked the steadily expanding prosperity of the preceding centuries. There were periods of acute depression and social unrest in all the great commercial and industrial cities during the fourteenth century. Some cities declined, while others grew. It is difficult to estimate how much the wealth of the cities actually increased during this period. There is, however, ample evidence of an increasing concentration of wealth and of a revolutionary development in the techniques of capitalist business enterprise. One result, the cultural and religious implications of which I shall return to later, was the spread of lay education in the cities; another, the growth of an urban patriciate composed of laymen who had the wealth, leisure, and cultivated taste to fit them for active participation in any form of intellectual or aesthetic culture. Still another result, the implications of which are more germane to my present argument, was the evolution by merchants, bankers, and financiers of new and more efficient methods of bookkeeping and accounting, as well as of more efficient techniques for the mobilization and transportation of money in large quantities. The development of state fiscal systems, the more rational accounting introduced into state chanceries, the hard-headed calculation behind the pious façade of royal policies, even the national bank-ruptcies that mark this period, are all evidence of the application to public finance of techniques and attitudes first worked out in the do-main of private capitalist enterprise.

All of these changes operated, directly or indirectly, to alter the character of medieval society; and, inasmuch as the Church had adapted itself with remarkable success to medieval conditions, any change was almost certain to be prejudicial to it. And, in fact, it did become increasingly difficult for the Church to maintain its dominant position in society and for the papacy to maintain the temporal supremacy it had won in the feudal era. At the same time, the papacy could not conceivably abandon without a struggle powers and privileges which the Church had possessed for centuries and had exercised for the good of the Christian community and for the salvation of souls. Not only would the abandonment of its traditional policy have involved encroachment upon too many vested interests; it would also have involved a grave dereliction of duty, the abdication of a responsibility for the moral government of Christendom that had been asserted by saints and popes and rationalized by centuries of canon law and scholastic argument. But to maintain its position under the new condi-tions, the government of the Church would have to fight with new weapons. It would have to meet the growing centralization of state administration with an increased centralization in the administration of the Church; and, as money became more and more the essential source of power, it would have to rival the fiscal system of state govern-ments by establishing a more efficient fiscal system of its own. Or so it must have seemed to anyone likely to achieve high office in the Church. There were mystics, like the spiritual Franciscans, who felt differently, and reformers, like John Wycliffe, whose conviction that wealth and power were a hindrance rather than a help to the Church drove them into heresy. But mystics are seldom successful politicians, even ecclesiastical politicians, and spiritually-minded reformers who advocated a return to apostolic poverty or the abandonment to Caesar of the things that were Caesar's were not likely to rise to positions of great authority in an institution committed to great possessions and to the exercise of temporal power. Yet the fiscal system and the concentration of administrative authority in the papal curia, both of which were developed with such skill by the fourteenth- and fifteenth-century popes, should not be considered simply the result of official will to power or avarice in high places. To the hierarchical mind there must have seemed no alternative. The changing policy of the Church as it strove to meet changing conditions must have seemed merely the continuation through new methods of the traditional policy of the preceding centuries. No Biblical injunction warned of the danger of putting old wine into new bottles.

Nevertheless, the development within the Church of a highly organized and centralized fiscal system implied more than the mere adaptation to old ends of a new means. Hitherto, the papal supremacy had been founded largely upon moral authority. The wealth of the Church had remained, even after the reintroduction of money economy, to a great extent decentralized. It was wealth drawn largely from land and held by the officers of the local church organization. By the end of the thirteenth century, however, the increased circulation of money, together with the growth of new techniques of bookkeeping, banking, and exchange, had made possible an effective system of taxation in both Church and state. Thereafter, the centralization of governmental authority and the elaboration of a fiscal system went hand in hand. In this the papacy was simply keeping pace with the secular governments. But the results were different, for the Church was not a secular institution devoted solely to secular ends, though its officers may occasionally have lost sight of this fact in their preoccupation with *Realpolitik* [practical politics]. The possession of wealth had always carried with it the threat of a materialism that might sap the spiritual vigor of the Church. Since the day of Peter Damiani preachers had complained that men were inspired to seek office in the Church by avarice and ambition. So long as the wealth of the Church remained decentralized, however, its central government had remained relatively uncontaminated. Under the new conditions not only the wealth but the materialism that went with it seemed to be concentrated in an unprecedented degree in the papal curia. Contemporary wits noticed that the word Roma furnished an acrostic base for the apothegm *radix omnium malorum avaritia* [root of all avaricious evils].

Nor did the danger end there, for the blight of fiscality spread throughout the Church. The increasing demands of the papal curia forced preoccupation with finance upon all the officers of the Church down to the parish level. And the effort of the papal chancery to introduce a fiscal system into an institution that had never been designed for it led inevitably to the systematization of simony and to traffic in spiritual goods. The fourteenth-century popes, it is true, were very largely successful in gaining that control of the nomination of prelates for which the medieval popes had labored in vain. But, as Dean Inge once remarked, in matters of religion nothing fails like success. The reservation to the papal curia of the right of nomination to vacant benefices throughout Christendom did not achieve a reform of the Church. On the contrary, fiscal pressures, diplomatic negotiations with secular princes, and nepotism in the curia made papal provisions the source of new abuses: absenteeism, duplication of offices, traffic in expectancies, the outright sale of benefices, and close calculation of the financial value of every office. Through the imposition of annates and *servitia* the system also imposed a crushing tax upon benefices, so that many of the charitable and other services expected of the local clergy were left undone. I need not describe here the fiscal expedients to which that financial genius, John XXII, and the other popes of this period resorted. Nor need I emphasize their deleterious effects upon clerical morality. These things are well enough known. Conditions were doubtless never as bad as the reforming preachers would have us believe. One cannot, however, entirely ignore the evidence of a cloud of witnesses to the effect that secular and material interests had done much to corrupt the spiritual character of the clergy, high and low. The pamphlet literature of the conciliar movement furnishes ample evidence of a widespread demand for reform of the Church in head and members, and of a growing conviction that reform could be achieved only by depriving the papal monarchy of some of its sovereign powers.

The conciliar movement, however, was by its very nature doomed to failure. Its constitutional theory ran counter to the trend of growing absolutism in the state as well as in the Church. The position of the bishops had been weakened by many of the same political and economic factors as had undermined the independence of the feudal nobles. The principle of free canonical election, for which the councils strove, had for centuries been no more than partially realized, and it was now a lost cause. It served the interest of the kings no more than of the popes. Finally, the whole conception of the ecumenical council as an international body governing a universal Church had become partially anachronistic. In practice, at any rate, it was vitiated by the intrusion of national governments, national interests, and national sentiments, which divided the councils and frustrated the attempt to impose a permanent control upon the papal executive.

The popes were thus able to weather the storm of the conciliar movement, and they emerged with their theoretical sovereignty intact and with a stronger hold than ever upon the administration of the Church. If so much was won, however, much also was lost. During the crisis years of the Captivity and the Schism the popes had gradually abandoned in practice their claims to supremacy over secular rulers. The fifteenth-century popes made their peace with kings and princes through a series of tacit agreements or formal concordats, by which they shared the nomination of church officers and the taxation of the clergy with the secular rulers. In England, the Statute of Provisors, which the fourteenth-century parliaments had used as an instrument to check papal provisions to English benefices, was allowed to become a dead letter. The English kings were content to leave to the popes the right of provision, and incidentally the annates or *servitia* paid by those who received their benefices by papal collation, on the tacit understanding that a certain number of royal ministers or favorites would be nominated. A similar tacit agreement to share some of the fruits of the papal right of provision in Germany with the emperor and the electors underlay the formal Concordat of Vienna of 1448, by means of which Nicholas V won the emperor Frederick III away from the Council of Basel. The French monarchy, long accustomed to special consideration by the Avignonese popes, proved more difficult to deal with. The Pragmatic Sanction of Bourges in 1438 was a unilateral assertion of the liberties of the Gallican Church, and for more than half a century it remained a threat to the principle of papal sovereignty. The theory of papal authority was finally saved by the Concordat of Bologna in 1516, but only at the cost of surrendering to Francis I the most profitable fruits of control of the national church.

In the system of concordats the papacy made its first adjustment to a world of strong secular states. The popes made such practical concessions as were necessary, without apparent impairment of their own *plenitudo potestatis*. For an estimate of the results we can scarcely do better than quote Professor McIlwain's masterly summary:

They were concessions only. But they were concessions guaranteed by a bilateral document in the nature of a treaty, which implies two treaty-making powers. The concordats were in fact the price the Papacy paid for its victory over the councils and it was a price heavier than appeared at the time. They were a tacit acknowledgement of the sovereignty of national states and they mark the virtual end of the medieval theory that Christendom in its secular aspect is one great state as in its spiritual it is a single Church. From such an admission the logical inference must come sooner or later that the Church is *in* every nation instead of embracing all nations, and this can ultimately mean only that its functions are primarily spiritual and that its participation in secular matters is never justifiable except for a spiritual end—*ad finem spiritualem*.[6]

[6] C. H. McIlwain, *The Growth of Political Thought in the West* (New York, 1932), p. 352.

That was undoubtedly the ultimate result; but it was not the moral immediately drawn from the situation by the popes in the century between the Council of Basel and the Council of Trent. Having failed to maintain the universal sovereignty that had been possible in the feudal age, they concentrated their attention upon restoring their temporal sovereignty in their own states. In this transitional stage, the popes became Italian princes. They suppressed the independent despotisms in the Papal States by force; they employed armies of mercenaries, waged wars, made and broke alliances, and in general took their place as one of the powers in the state system of Europe. In this period political expediency dominated papal policy, though fiscal considerations were not neglected. The College of Cardinals now included members of the ruling families of Italy and the chief ministers of the great European states. Never before had the papacy seemed so securely established as a temporal power, but never before had its power seemed so purely temporal as it did in the age of Alexander VI and Julius II. This was its period of greatest peril. On the one hand the pope, as temporal ruler of the states of the Church, was no more than a third-rate power, on the level more or less of Milan or Florence. In the game of power politics he was no match for France or Spain. In 1527 the papacy that had chosen to live by the sword came very close to perishing by the sword, and thereafter the popes, as temporal rulers, were drawn into the Spanish sphere of influence, becoming satellites whose foreign policy was dominated by Spanish kings. On the other hand, the preoccupation of the papal curia with temporal politics during these crisis years made it peculiarly unfitted to combat the spiritual revolution that broke out in Germany and that, within two generations, separated half of northern Europe permanently from the Church of Rome. The papacy survived this crisis too, with its sovereignty over what remained of the Church strengthened rather than weakened; but it did so only by ceasing to compete with secular states upon their own terms, by withdrawing into the spiritual sphere in which its authority was unchallenged, by restating the doctrines of the Church in the spirit of the great scholastic age, by employing the militia of the Society of Jesus rather than hired mercenaries, and by leaving coercive jurisdiction to the secular arm of state governments.

So far I have concentrated attention primarily upon the papacy and the Church in their relation to the secular states. That, however, is only a part of the problem of assessing the position of the Church in the changing civilization of the Renaissance. The relation of the Church to contemporary changes in culture, religious sentiment, and

general *Weltanschauung* is of equal if not greater importance, but it
is less easy to summarize in a brief paper. Here I can do no more than
make a few general observations.

One factor of primary importance for the whole cultural evolution
of the Renaissance period, it seems to me, was the growth of lay education. This was not an entirely unknown phenomenon in the Middle
Ages. As James Westfall Thompson and others have demonstrated,
there was more literacy, at least among medieval laymen than historians
used to suppose, though that is not saying very much.[7] Nevertheless,
the magnificent intellectual and aesthetic achievements of the twelfth
and thirteenth centuries, if we exclude the vernacular literature of
chivalry, was almost entirely the work of clerics and was patronized,
organized, and directed by the Church *ad majorem Dei gloriam* [to the
greater glory of God]. Under feudal conditions the nobles had little
use for learning and less for art, while the burghers had not yet acquired
the wealth, social security, or independent cultural tradition that would
enable them to compete with the clergy in this sphere. In Italy, however,
before the end of the thirteenth century, and in other countries of
western Europe somewhat later, the social and economic development
of the cities had reached a point where literacy was a necessity, and
higher education a possibility, for the middle and upper classes of the
urban population. To this end the growth of communal governments
staffed by lay administrators, increasing prosperity, and the gradual
evolution of a more self-confident burgher tradition all contributed.
But on a purely material level the major factor, I think, was the expansion of business enterprise which accompanied the transition from
itinerant to sedentary commerce, and the growth of capitalist forms of
business organization. This involved, on the one hand, bookkeeping,
written instruments of credit and exchange, accurate calculation of
profit and loss, complicated negotiations with distant agents or partners,
and a much more precise definition of civil law, all of which made
literacy indispensable for everyone connected with business in any
managerial capacity and also called into being a numerous learned class
of lay lawyers, scribes, and notaries. On the other hand, it resulted
in the concentration of wealth and the accumulation of surplus capital
which furnished the means for lay patronage of literature, learning, and
the arts. It also created a new class of leisured *rentiers,* who lived on inherited wealth and were free to devote themselves to intellectual or
aesthetic interests. The concentration of both wealth and political power

[7] J. W. Thompson, *The Literacy of the Laity in the Middle Ages* (Berkeley,
1939).

in royal or princely courts served the same purpose in slightly different ways. Such courts became the centers for the patronage and dissemination of lay culture, and so exposed the courtly nobility to a wider range of cultural interests than had been available in the isolated baronial castles of the feudal era. After 1450 the invention of printing vastly increased the lay reading public and tipped the scale decisively in favor of lay participation in all forms of literary culture; but that epoch-making invention was itself the answer to a demand already large enough to ensure its being a profitable venture.

The spread of lay education and lay patronage and the growth of a distinct class of lay men of letters greatly expanded the secular content of Renaissance culture. This does not imply any necessary decline in religious sentiment. On the contrary, it was accompanied in many places by a pronounced growth in lay piety. Nevertheless, it was detrimental in many ways to the dominant position which the Church had acquired in medieval society. It deprived the Church of its exclusive control of higher education and the clergy of their monopoly of learning and serious thought. And it created a rival, if not an antagonist, to the ecclesiastical culture of the preceding centuries. Evidence of this may be found everywhere in Renaissance music and art, as well as in literature and learning. The revival of antiquity is but one aspect, if the most prominent, of this general trend. Humanism grew up largely as a lay interest, the offspring of lay education, though many humanists were technically clerics. It was, at any rate, not controlled and directed by the Church as scholasticism had been, and it may even be said to have imposed itself upon the Church in the person of such popes as Nicholas V and Pius II and the scores of humanists highly placed in the ecclesiastical hierarchy. In the long run, humanism of the Erasmian variety inspired the most telling attacks upon the temporal power, wealth, and materialism of the Church in the period just preceding the Protestant Reformation.

The reforming Christian humanism of the Erasmian circle represents another aspect of the danger to the medieval Church inherent in the spread of lay education. As I noted in passing, this was accompanied in many places by a distinct revival of lay piety. But the lay piety inspired by mystical preachers like Eckhart and Tauler, and represented by such movements as that of the Friends of God in the Rhineland or the *Devotio Moderna* in the Netherlands, was in large part a reaction against the sacerdotalism of the Church, its mechanization of the means of salvation and the materialism of the contemporary clergy. It is clear that in these years of crisis the Church was not satisfying the spiritual needs of many thoughtful and pious laymen. Left to find their own way toward a sense of personal communion with Christ, they read the New Testament and devotional works which, while entirely orthodox, still had the effect of shifting the emphasis in religious thought from the services of the Church to the inner life of faith and a loving devotion to the person of Christ. It was this peculiarly lay piety that Erasmus, who had been taught in his early years by the Brethren of the Common Life, introduced to a wide circle of educated readers in the *Enchiridion Militis Christiani* and a score of other works less ostensibly devotional.

It may be, too, that the growing bourgeois ethic . . . was in these centuries drifting away from the moral teaching and ascetic ideals of the medieval Church. The pious burgher, sober and hard-working, may well have resented the attitude of the doctors of the Church who barely tolerated commercial activity; and he may also have been tempted to regard the monks, especially such monks as he saw about him, as men who had not so much fled the pleasures and temptations of the world as escaped from its responsibilities. Finally, the intellectual independence which education gave to laymen, together with the individualism fostered by a complex and changing society, might well have made men less ready to accept without question the absolute authority of the Church in matters of doctrine or the claim of the clergy to be the indispensable purveyors of the means of salvation. There has, I think, been a good deal of confused thinking concerning the relationship of capitalism to Protestantism. Nevertheless, I think there can be little doubt that the economic and social conditions which made possible a widespread lay literacy and stimulated a growing sense of self-confident individualism did, at the same time, create an intellectual and moral atmosphere favorable to the reception of Luther's doctrine of the freedom of a Christian man and the priesthood of all believers.

Consideration of the Protestant Reformation, however, except as it affected the Catholic Church, lies beyond the scope of the present discussion. The Church survived this crisis also, with its membership sadly diminished but with its divinely inspired authority strongly reaffirmed. Though papal infallibility was not yet a dogma, the popes after Trent enjoyed an absolute authority in matters of faith and morals greater than that of even their most authoritative medieval predecessors. In the cultural and religious, as well as in the political and administrative fields, the Counter-Reformation completed the Church's adjustment to the modern world. Since then it has changed but relatively little. Yet, if I have assessed aright the predominant characteristics of modern civilization, it was no more than a partial adjustment, and was in some respects a reaction. It was certainly no surrender to the new elements that had grown up within Western civilization since the High Middle Ages. It was rather an orderly retreat to a previously prepared position. The withdrawal of the Church into the spiritual sphere in which its authority could still be exercised in absolute fashion involved not only the abdication of temporal supremacy but also the partial rejection of the secular philosophies, the natural sciences, and large areas of the autonomous lay culture that grew out of the Renaissance. While making concessions where concessions were unavoidable, and abandoning such claims to authority in secular matters as changing conditions had made untenable, the Church returned after the Counter-Reformation, though in a more purely spiritual sense, to the conception of its nature and function that had been formulated in the twelfth and thirteenth centuries. What it could not dominate it rejected, and so maintained, in an ever-shrinking sphere, the authoritative direction of human activity that, in the Middle Ages, had approached a universal domination of the temporal as well as the spiritual life of the Christian community.

But if the Church thus finally succeeded in adapting the medieval ideal to the realities of the modern world, it did so only after a series of well-nigh disastrous crises, which lend to its history during the transitional period a special character. If we consider the events and the changes in ecclesiastical polity that fill the years between the death of Boniface VIII and the period of reconstruction after the Council of Trent, and if we take as the common factor in all of them the efforts, often misguided or self-defeating, of the Church and the papacy to maintain the position they had achieved during the Middle Ages in the midst of a social complex that was being radically altered by new economic, political, and cultural forces, we may, I think, safely conclude that the three centuries of the Renaissance constitute a distinct period in Church history, and that to treat them as such will serve to clarify much that might otherwise remain obscure. The Renaissance Church and the Renaissance papacy were neither medieval nor modern; rather they were caught in a state of uneasy maladjustment between two worlds. It is the distinguishing mark of a genuinely transitional period that the unresolved conflict between traditional institutions and ways of thinking on the one hand, and, on the other, changing economic, political, and social conditions creates a state of acute crisis. The Renaissance was such a period, and the effects of the conflict, as well as the fundamental causes, are, I believe, nowhere more clearly evident than in the history of the Church.

BIBLIOGRAPHY

Leonard Elliott-Binns, *The History of the Decline and Fall of the Medieval Papacy* (London: 1934). Wallace K. Ferguson, *Europe in Transition, 1300–1520* (Boston: 1963); *The Renaissance in Historical Thought* (Boston: 1949). Myron P. Gilmore, *The World of Humanism, 1453–1517* (New York: 1952). Henry S. Lucas, *The Renaissance and the Reformation*, 2nd ed. (New York: 1960). Pierre Janelle, *The Catholic Reformation* (Milwaukee: 1949). Hubert Jedin, *A History of the Council of Trent* (2 vols.; London: 1957–61). Ludwig von Pastor, *The History of the Popes from the Close of the Middle Ages* (vols. 1–40; London and St. Louis: 1891 ff.). William Pauck, "The Idea of the Church in Christian History," *Church History*, XXI (1952), 191–214. S. Harrison Thomson, *Europe in Renaissance and Reformation* (New York: 1963). [The Editor.]

WHY THE REFORMATION OCCURRED IN GERMANY *

Gerhard Ritter

One of the great puzzles of historical speculation, since its occurence more than four and one-half centuries ago, is why the religious uprising against the medieval Church sparked by Martin Luther occurred. But more, why did it happen first in Germany and why was Luther successful when many other medieval dissenters from the Church's teachings had failed? Whether we can ever have complete and satisfactory answers to these questions is perhaps doubtful. Such explanations lie almost beyond the ken of historical knowledge. Nonetheless, much may be adduced from existing evidence, and Professor Gerhard Ritter has done so in the following selection.

* Reprinted with the permission of the author and the editors of *Church History* (XXVII, 1958, 99–106).

Translated from the original "Kirche und geistiges Leben in Deutschland um 1517," (Chap. 8 of the author's *Die Neugestaltung Europas im 16. Jahrhundert*, Berlin, 1950) by G. H. Nadel.

At the end of the Middle Ages, the moral prestige of the old papal church was severely shaken in all the countries of Europe. Open criticism of its moral shortcomings and its organizational defects had been going on for centuries. To the diverse splinter-movements of heretical sects (which were never wholly suppressed) had been recently added the great reform movements of the Wyclifites and the Hussites. But even they had brought about no lasting and widespread upheaval. Ultimately the old hierarchy had always prevailed. Why then did the Germans, a people slow to be aroused, fond of order, and faithful to the church, take it upon themselves to carry out the most prodigious revolution in the church? And why did only their revolt against the papal church have such vast and enduring consequences?

By way of answer, it is of course not enough to cite the adverse outcome of the council proceedings, particularly in Germany, the "gravamina of the German nation," and the reformatory efforts of the German territorial governing bodies. For those complaints and reform efforts made no headway in the direction in which the Lutheran Reformation was later to move—towards a renewal of church life in its innermost regions, one which would start from a new understanding of the Christian revelation rather than from patchwork improvement of the outward deficiencies of the ecclesiastical system.

It is true that this decisively new impetus to reform was entirely the personal deed of an individual of genius, without example or precedent: the deed of Martin Luther. But how did it happen that in Germany it was not immediately branded as heresy and stamped out, but met with a loud response, which did not even abate when it became universally evident that the attack shook the dogmatic foundations of the old priestly church? Could this response perhaps become intelligible in the light of the special nature of German Christian piety?

A person coming at this time across the Alps from Italy would sense immediately the vastly greater intensity of ecclesiastical and religious life among the Germans. The secularization of existence, the fading of the Christian ascetic ideals of the Middle Ages, encountered at the Renaissance courts of the South are not yet felt. All life is still consummated in the shadow of the mighty cathedrals, which dominate the panorama of the German city. With unbroken force the Christian teaching of the world to come still determines all forms of life; its influence, indeed, seems to wax continuously. Pious foundations become alarmingly numerous. Hundreds of clerical benefices, many dozens of altars, accumulate in the great churches; in Cologne, a good third of built-up ground was said to have been church property, and in some other places every tenth inhabitant was said to have belonged to the clergy. The sumptuous furnishings even of small village churches and the daily influx of churchgoers never cease to astound foreign travelers. The ecclesiastical organization of the masses pushes rapidly ahead. All kinds of lay brotherhoods, for the care of the poor and the sick, for the erection of homes, for common devotions, increase in number and magnitude with extraordinary speed. Every mendicant order attracts such associations; but still others spring up like weeds, and their spiritual control and supervision cause the church authorities no little concern. These groups teach their members unselfish service of their neighbors, but at the same time an outward sanctimoniousness which is shrewdly calculated to secure for itself certain salvation in the next world by multiplying prayers and oblations. Church devotions have become popular, the most sacred has become commonplace; very often, religious excitation is combined with a rank mania for sensation and miracle. The system of pilgrimages and relics, with its thousand frauds, the spread of the belief in witches, the alarming frequency of religious epidemics, of eschatological states of excitement in the masses—all these are repellent enough. But who could on their account overlook the numerous testimonies of profound and genuine piety, the deep poetic touches of the cult of Mary with its reflections in poetry and the plastic arts and the moral effects of spreading the church's teachings among the people?

Now what is peculiar is how closely this very vigorous popular piety is combined with severe, even embittered, criticism of the church and of her clergy; this attitude contrasts very noticeably with the blind devotion of the Spanish masses to the church. This criticism, voiced with equal severity among all classes of the German people, is itself a testimony, not perhaps of diminishing, but rather of live and increasing interest in religion and the church. There is, indeed, nothing which excites public opinion more than the church and its preaching. Among the masses, and in particular among the peasants, the preaching of the radical mendicant friars of the ideal of the propertyless church, in contrast to the prelates grown rich and unscrupulous, is most effective; in the agitation carried on by nameless hole-and-corner preachers, this ideal is not infrequently combined with communistic ideas in the style of the Hussites and with apocalyptic expectations of the imminent end of the world. Among the urban middle classes there is primarily the sound common-sense criticism of excessive church privileges and of the contradiction between the claims of the clergy to spiritual authority and its scandalous manner of life; finally, there is also the misuse of mass devotion by the sellers of relics and indulgences, whose fraudulent practices do not deceive the burgher's sober business sense. The lazy dronelike existence of monastics and of so many recipients of church benefices arouses the ire of the diligent artisan; the democratic consciousness of the new age offers resistance to the aristocratic, dignified, and contemplative mode of life of the higher clergy. The burgher is also apt to be critical of the overly artful scholastic sermon whose content is often overloaded with theological subtleties, of the involved casuistry of canon law and its procedures of penance; he desires an unsophisticated form of Christian teaching accessible to all, a straightforward handling, intelligible to the layman, of the church's authority to punish. The noble too has his bitter complaints against papal administration of benefices and financial practices. And finally, among men of letters—that is to say, above all among the members of universities, academic graduates, the more studious clerics, and certain of the urban patriciate—the Humanists' criticism of church tradition gradually gains ground.

For in Germany too the reverence of the Italian Humanists for classical greatness of soul, for the beauty of classical forms of life, art, and poetry, found enthusiastic followers. At princely courts here and there, in the patrician houses of the great south-German imperial cities, and at most of the universities, the imitation of Italian patronage of arts and letters, of Italian 'academies' and literary circles was begun; letters and poems were exchanged in artful and laboriously turned Latin; old authors, ancient coins, and all sorts of antiquities were unearthed and collected. The best fruit of these scholarly and semi-scholarly efforts was a literature which for the first time sought after the historical origin of the German character. It traced and published German historical sources of the Middle Ages, collected old-German folk-customs, proverbs, and the like, and created an ideal of a genuine Germanic character which in its essentials went back to the *Germania* of Tacitus. Together with this went all kinds of empty rhetoric, false pathos, courtly flattery (especially in the service of the house of Habsburg), fanciful creation of legends, and even deliberate falsification of history. Yet German national historiography received its first strong impetus from the semi-dilettante efforts of Celtis, Cuspinian, Trithemius, Wimpfeling, Bebel, Nauclerus, Peutinger, Pirckheimer, and many others. Chroniclers like Aventin and scholarly antiquaries like Beatus Rhenanus rose far above the craft of the medieval chronicler. Such juridical learning as Ulrich Zasius' and Bonifacius Amerbach's challenged for the first time the heretofore undoubted preeminence of the Italian jurists. Cosmographers like Sebastian Münster and Martin Waldseemüller, orientalists like Reuchlin and Pellican founded new branches of learning. The rigid formula of scholastic tradition was attacked from all possible angles, and ample scope was obtained for new branches of knowledge, for a new, freer view of the world. All this added considerably to the strengthening of the national self-consciousness of educated Germans. They would no longer allow themselves to be called 'barbarians' by the Southern people. It became a favorite theme of patriotic literature to praise the ancient virtues of the German character by calling on Tacitus and to contrast German bravery and fidelity with Latin cunning and frivolity. Thus humanistic literature soon gained a keenly nationalistic trait. It turned against the "hereditary enemy," France, in the service of imperial foreign politics, and against the Roman curia, in the service of the German imperial estates and their 'gravamina'. But it met invariably with greatest approval when it treated the favorite theme of the time: the faults of the church.

The Humanists' own contribution to this theme was chiefly the derision of the paltry education of the average cleric. There was mockery of the 'barbarous' Latin, the peasant-like bearing, and the 'stinking cowls' of the mendicant friars, and the like, closely combined, naturally, with the usual jokes on concubinage, public immorality, and the high living of the priests. The most pointed satire of this kind was the collection of the fictitious 'Dunkelmännerbriefe',[1] produced by Hutten's circle of friends. In it the new literary estate, whose self-respect was severely offended by the church's censorship of the great scholar Reuchlin and of his propaganda for Hebrew literature, gave vent to its need for vengeance in quite unmeasured and obscene terms. Among the criticism of the church must also be reckoned the Humanists' fight against scholastic learning and theology with its empty subtleties and artificialities. But this fight remained fruitless as long as it would merely destroy without erecting a truly all-embracing new ideal of learning and culture which went beyond the introduction of new style forms and new academic subjects (such as Greek and Hebrew grammar). Only two of the Humanists on German soil, however, were capable of this: Rudolf Agricola, who died in his youth in 1485, and Desiderius Erasmus. Both belonged to the cultural circle of the Netherlands.

What the German Humanists at once understood and took from the life-work of the great Dutchman was first its satirical, condescending criticism of the outward aspect of the late medieval church: the scan-

---

[1] *Letters of Obscure Men.* [Editor's note.]

dalous mode of life and ignorance of her priests, especially of the monks, the dull superstition of the populace, the excess of her ritual, her misuse of spiritual power for secular purposes, and the degeneration of her theological learning. In his *Praise of Folly* he could put more cleverly and aptly than anyone else the doubts and objections which the sound common sense of the German burgher had long raised. The new wide outlook on the world and on life which stood behind this admittedly went over the heads of most German readers as far as its final aims were concerned. It was the ideal of an intimate union of humane and liberal culture, of humanity in the sense of the old Hellenic and old Roman patrician society, with the Christian ethic of love as defined in Jesus' Sermon on the Mount. The 'philosophy of Christ', as Erasmus imagined it, set out to reconcile the consciousness of the natural dignity and moral strength of man, newly sprung up in Italy, with the teaching of Christ's act of redemption and our duty to follow it; it set out to unite the belief in the unique value of the Christian revelation with the recognition of religious truth in the great spiritual creations of all peoples and all times. This was possible only with the aid of many ambiguous, often contradictory, theological formulations which barred the great mass of German readers from a deeper understanding of the Erasmian ideals of life. They exercised their strongest influence outside territorial Germany: we shall meet them in the path of the Swiss and Dutch Reformation and also repeatedly in the Latin countries and in England. Erasmus was in any event far removed from the emphatic nationalism of the German Humanists and from their crude contentiousness; he lived in a cosmopolitan world of learning beyond all nationalistic boundaries and shunned nothing more than any threatened intrusion of the noise of great political struggles into the edifying calm of his scholarly existence. If in Germany he was despite this hailed with extravagant enthusiasm as leader, indeed as prophet and champion of a new age, this was largely a misunderstanding. Erasmus' tender, subdued philosophy of life and his dignified and delicate scholar's personality were not made for the severe and decisive spiritual and political battles towards which Germany now advanced. Yet his theology showed certain genuinely German traits, which separate him clearly from Italian Humanism and which help to explain the astonishingly powerful effort he had on Germany despite all his cool cosmopolitan restraint.

In order to understand the special nature of the German piety of that time in contrast to other forms of worship, particularly the Latin, one might best begin with a comparison of religious works of art. What is obscured in theological literature, dominated as it must be by the universal ideas and thought-forms of scholasticism, immediately becomes visible in art: the striving of the German temper for a direct personal appropriation of salvation. Italian religious art preferred scenes of the glorification of the church, her means of grace, her holy fathers and martyrs, and her triumphs; it liked to represent the Mother of God as a princely personage, surrounded where possible by her heavenly retinue. Altar pictures of this kind are found in Germany too, but far more popular are representations of a more intimate kind which move the pious heart: scenes, perhaps, from the life of Mary, with pictures in a middle-class setting, but especially Christ's passion, depicted with the most intimate participation in the suffering of the Man of Sorrows. The *Vesperbild* or *Pietà*, the representation of the Mother of Sorrows with the dead Son on her knee, is the only German contribution to the rich treasury of motives of late medieval religious art. The Last Judgment, too, with its horror, and the story of the wise and the foolish virgins, with its strong appeal to conscience, never failed to move German artists very deeply.

Even this cursory observation indicates intellectual and spiritual connections which it would be easy to confirm by further examples and to trace through the entire Middle Ages. Time and again a buried antagonism comes to light, a contest between the spirit of Latin churchdom, with its outward legalism, and German piety, with its strong temperamental needs and intense seriousness of conscience. Throughout the Middle Ages, the Roman church developed more markedly into a legal institution, whose rigid juridical-theological apparatus bound the religious procedure of salvation increasingly to the execution of outward sacred acts and the fulfillment of external sacred norms. But this very development serves to conceal even further the genuine, pristine essence of religion as the direct personal experience of God. The conscience of the deepest and purest German spirits had already revolted against this in the Middle Ages. Outward exhibition of religious experience in glowing ecstasies and visions, in new and striking forms of monastic asceticism, had always been rarer in Germany than the tendency to the most intimate submersion in the divine secrets. None of the founders of the great medieval orders was a German. There was, however, a German mysticism of great historical significance, which can be traced throughout the entire late Middle Ages.

The lay piety of upper Germany and the Netherlands (in which Erasmus too was nurtured), now turning towards more mystic edification, now towards more practical and efficacious piety, shows a common trend in its most varied forms: to relegate the church's sacramental apparatus of grace to lesser importance than the personal assurance of salvation which is sought and experienced by the individual believer in direct intercourse with his God. This, of course, need by no means lead to an attitude of opposition to the church. But the more emphatically the church stressed the indispensability of priestly mediation and juridically extended the concept of the power of the keys, the closer lay the danger that the pious soul would feel this intervention as a disturbing impediment, as an interference of alien power in the innermost secrets of the heart. The boundary between mysticism and heresy was never clearly drawn and was easily transgressed; indeed Germany in the fifteenth century was almost overflowing with mystical heretical sects. And even among the great mass of church people, where heretical inclinations were lacking, the priestly performance of the sacraments could be regarded more or less indifferently and pushed aside. The more easily this was done, the lower the moral prestige of the priesthood sank, and the misuse of the power of the keys for secular purposes became manifest. Finally, there was no lack of opposition-minded reformers who were able to justify on theological grounds such a rejection or at least devaluation of priestly mediation in salvation. In the writings of the so-called 'early reformers', especially of the Dutchman Wessel Gansfort, one can already discover a revolutionary bent which resembles the Lutheran conception of the process of salvation. Also outside the mystic tradition, Wyclifite ideas, which proposed to set a new community of saints in place of the hierarchically conceived priestly church, continually excited and engaged German theologians. The conviction that all reform in theology must begin with a return to the oldest and most original truths of Christianity, intelligible to the layman, was disseminated in the widest circles; it too was among the basic teachings of Erasmus and through the instrumentality of his writings it took hold of a very broad stratum of scholars, theological as well as lay. On the eve of the Reformation there were throughout Germany pious men and women to whom, from the point of view of their personal faith, the church with its splendid hierarchy appeared as a place of downright sale and corruption. They lived in a religion of quiet inwardness, in uncertain groping and seeking, of which hardly anything was expressed publicly. But because here was undoubtedly the greatest religious vitality, they too constituted a dangerous threat to the dominance of the old church. It was only a matter of combining the new religious vitality of the 'devout in the land' with the already mentioned loud criticism and political opposition, which filled the whole age, against the outward aspects of the church. Once this combination had been accomplished the revolutionary momentum could no longer be arrested.

In retrospect we see both currents of church opposition at work simultaneously though at first independently. The one struggles against manifest abuses and insists on reforms, but in practice does not go beyond a patchwork improvement of institutions. Though it does not reach down into spiritual depths, it is nevertheless most impassioned, impelling, and popular. The other current is less concerned with the outward appearance of the church, but instead touches on the substance of religion and the spiritual roots of church life. Those in power long underestimate its significance because at first it lacks any prospect of practical effect. But at the same time, it has the advantage that practical power can do nothing against it. In the figure of Martin Luther the two currents combine for the first time. He is a man of the people, an agitator in grandest style, and the most popular speaker and writer that Germany has ever produced; possessed of unprecedented hitting power and coarseness of language, of boundless anger and fighting zeal, he sways the masses most forcefully. He shares the moral indignation of his contemporaries over the outward corruption of the church; he uses all the slogans of anticlerical and antipapal opposition of the preceding hundred years and still outdoes them—but at the same time he is the most brilliant and profound theological thinker, the most powerful and strong-willed prophet-figure of his people, and a religious genius whose experience of faith is of unprecedented inwardness and intimacy.

This combination is plainly unique. And thus Luther became incomparably the most formidable opponent of the old church.

BIBLIOGRAPHY

General works: Roland Bainton, *The Reformation of the Sixteenth Century* (Boston: 1952). G. R. Elton, *Reformation Europe, 1517–1559* (London: 1963). Harold J. Grimm, *The Reformation Era, 1500–1660* (New York: 1954). E. Harris Harbison, *The Age of the Reformation* (Ithaca, N.Y.: 1955). Mgr. Philip Hughes, *A Popular History of the Reformation* (Garden City, N.Y.: 1957). George L. Mosse, *The Reformation* (New York: 1953). William Pauck, *The Heritage of the Reformation* (rev. and enl. ed.; Glencoe, Ill.: 1961). Lewis Spitz (ed.), *The Reformation* (Boston: 1962). T. F. Torrance, *Kingdom and Church. A Study in the Theology of the Reformation* (London: 1956). Lutheranism: Roland Bainton, *Here I Stand. A Life of Martin Luther* (New York, 1955). John

Dillenberger, *God Hidden and Revealed* [Theology] (Philadelphia: 1953).
Robert H. Fife, *The Revolt of Martin Luther* (New York: 1957). B. A.
Gerrish, *Grace and Reason* [Theology] (Oxford: 1962). Hajo Holborn, *A
History of Modern Germany. The Reformation* (New York: 1959). E.
Gordon Rupp, *The Righteousness of God* [Theology] (London: 1953).
Ernest G. Schwiebert, *Luther and His Times* (St. Louis: 1950). Calvinism:
Edward A. Dowey, Jr., *The Knowledge of God in the Theology of Calvin*
(New York: 1952). John T. McNeill, *The History and Character of
Calvinism* (New York: 1954). T. H. L. Parker, *The Doctrine of the Knowl-
edge of God* [Theology] (Edinburgh: 1952); *Portrait of Calvin* (London,
n. d.). Francois Wendel, *Calvin* (London: 1963). [The Editor.]

CALVINISM, CAPITALISM, AND THE MIDDLE CLASSES: SOME AFTERTHOUGHTS ON AN OLD PROBLEM *

Sidney A. Burrell

*The following two selections are included in this series because they
deal with one of the most provocative questions in modern historiography, namely, whether there was an intrinsic connection between the
religious ideas of the Protestant reformers and the rise of modern capitalism. The existence of such a connection has come to be so widely accepted that it is even included in much of the general and textbook literature on the Reformation. The Burrell excerpt briefly traces the history of
the conception and the controversy stemming from it. Professor Hudson
examines the conception critically in the light of expanded scholarly
knowledge since the idea was first put forward by the German soci
ologist, Max Weber, more than half a century ago.*

Among the widely accepted conventions of modern historiography
few have been more tenaciously held or more strongly criticized than
the assumption that Protestantism, particularly in its Calvinist form,
emerged in the sixteenth century as the ideology of a "rising middle
class." Like most well-established, conventionalized forms of thought

* Reprinted with the permission of the University of Chicago Press and the
editors of *The Journal of Modern History* (XXXII, 1960, 129–141, with omissions).

this one has been difficult to displace in recent historical thinking because it has for long been supported by the researches of a number of eminent and able scholars whose conclusions are reinforced and seemingly confirmed by the verisimilitude of an observable historical connection. Calvinism, after all, did have its beginnings in the city-state of Geneva; and as it spread across Northern and Western Europe during the sixteenth and seventeenth centuries it seemed to grow best in those areas where commercial activity and urban life were most flourishing. Nothing has seemed more natural, therefore, than to assume that there must have been a close, nexus-like affinity between Calvinism and commerce or, more broadly, between Calvinism and that expanding capitalism which has always been regarded as the peculiar economic attribute of the European bourgeoisie.

Let us begin by looking briefly at the historiographical development of the idea that Calvinism is the ideology of the capitalistic middle class. Curiously enough, the origin of this belief actually goes back to the sixteenth century when it first took form in the argument between Anglicans and Presbyterians over church government. In response to the claims of the Elizabethan Presbyterians, who asserted that rule by presbyteries rather than by bishops was proper for Christ's church, Anglican defenders of the Elizabethan establishment like Archbishop John Whitgift countered with the assertion that, while elderships and presbyteries were well suited to the life of city-states and towns, episcopacy was the only useful and proper ecclesiastical polity for large kingdoms. During the next sixty years this assertion proved so useful to the Anglican cause that Presbyterians were driven to make the highest *jure divino* claims for their system. It was not, they declared, "a Lesbian rule answerable to any form of civil polity" but that ecclesiastical government truly intended for the salvation of all mankind because it was "best warranted by the Word of God." In its most extreme form this latter claim was put forth by the supporters of the Scottish Covenant whose revolt against Charles I, which began in 1637, took on the aspect of a vast Presbyterian crusade whose aim was to establish, first, a kind of British theocracy and, ultimately, a universal, presbyterianized Christian church. With stubborn insistence, however, their opponents, unimpressed by the exalted nature of these claims, continued to assert that the Calvinist-Presbyterian system was a religion better suited to "mercantile republicks and cantoned towns rather than to great kingdoms."

Despite the vehemence of their protestations, the verdict of later historiography went against the Scottish Covenanters and other Calvinists who shared their views. During the eighteenth century, when religious fervor had somewhat cooled, another generation of thinkers swayed by different influences, looked back to the civil wars of the preceding century and saw them not as struggles for the restoration of Christ's earthly kingdom nor even as great contests for the liberties of the subject but as power conflicts rooted in economic and class enmity. The reason for this transformation is not far to seek. After 1750, with the rise in prestige of that new tool of social analysis known as "political economy," an ever larger number of persons sought to test it against historical fact. By a kind of ironic twist, it was Calvinist Scotland which produced two of these early historical sociologists, James Steuart of Coltness, better known for his economic treatises, and John Millar, an academic colleague of Adam Smith at the University of Glasgow. Like Smith, both men saw deep significance in certain economic developments of the preceding hundred years. It has been suggested that Millar, in particular, was actually a forerunner of the nineteenth-century school of Marxian sociology.[1] This claim is exaggerated, for much of his thought derived from the premises of a rather conventional eighteenth-century rationalism, but the assertion does have a measure of truth. By implication at least, both men seemed to argue that economic change preceded and caused political change. In the view of Steuart of Coltness, for example, the downfall of the feudal aristocracy throughout Europe was a result of fundamental shifts in the economic relations which had controlled European life for centuries.

In countries [he wrote] where the government is vested in the hands of the great lords, as is the case in all aristocracies, as was the case under the feudal government, and as it still is the case in many countries of Europe, where trade, however, and industry are daily gaining ground; the stateseman who sets the new system of political economy on foot, may depend upon it, either his attempt will fail, or the constitution of the government will change. If he destroys all arbitrary dependence between individuals, the wealth of the industrious will share, if not totally root out the power of the grandees.[2]

In this and in one or two other respects it must be admitted that there were latent in the thought of Steuart ideas which Marx was to develop more fully toward somewhat different conclusions in the century following. Steuart believed not only that men were motivated and

---

[1] See Ronald L. Meek, "The Scottish contribution to Marxian Sociology" in John Saville (ed.), *Democracy and the labour movement* (London, 1954).

[2] James Steuart of Coltness, *Works, political, metaphisical, and chronological* (London, 1805), I, 327.

controlled to a large extent by economic necessity but that the possession of wealth automatically brought with it political power. Like
Marx, Steuart also concluded that changes in the methods of production altered existing social relationships and aroused class hostilities,
though he did not regard this eventuality as an inevitable law of
history.[3]

Steuart's thought, though important for its contribution to the general climate of European opinion, was by no means unique; nor was it
quite so explicitly pointed in the direction of later Marxian thought
as that of Millar whose views seem to foreshadow Marx's own contribution to nineteenth-century historical and sociological theory. Millar
formulated a fairly well thought out proto-Marxian interpretation of
history in which he called attention to the prime importance of class
distinctions and antagonisms. It is to Millar, for example, that we
owe what may be the first attempt to explain the English civil wars as
class struggles. His explanation of the reasons for division between the
supporters of the king and those of parliament is one which a number
of historians would find acceptable today. As he saw it:

> The adherents of the king were chiefly composed of the nobility and
> higher gentry, men who, by their wealth and station had much to lose; and
> who, in the annihilation of monarchy, and in the anarchy that was likely
> to follow, foresaw the ruin of their consideration and influence. The
> middling and inferior gentry, together with the inhabitants of the towns;
> those who entertained a jealousy of the nobles, and of the king, or who,
> by the changes in the state of society, had lately been raised to independence,
> became, on the other hand the great supporters of parliament, and formed
> the chief part of the armies levied by that assembly.[4]

While it is uncertain how much Marx, Engels, or other members
of the Marxian school may have read of the writing of Steuart or
Millar, we do know that Marx himself was led to the conviction that
the class struggle was the central theme of history by persons whom he
described as "bourgeois historians." [5] Marx, however, did make an

---

[3] "From reason it is plain that industry must give wealth, and wealth *will*
give power, if he who possesses it be left the master to employ it as he pleases.
. . . It was consequently very natural of the nobility to be jealous of the wealthy
merchants, and of every one who became easy and independent by means of
his own industry; experience proved how exactly this principle regulated their
administration." *Ibid.*, I, 326.

[4] John Millar, *An historical view of the English government* (London, 1812),
III, 295.

[5] See Marx's acknowledgment in an oft-quoted letter to Weydemeyer, March
5, 1852, contained in Dona Torr (ed.), *Karl Marx and Friedrich Engels, Correspondence, 1846–1895* (New York, 1934), p. 57.

important original contribution to the development of modern historiography and historical sociology by explicitly calling attention to the relationship between social conditions and the non-material manifestations of human activity in the form of beliefs and ideas for which Karl Mannheim has credited him with the discovery of the "sociology of knowledge." His conclusions as set forth in the introduction to his *Critique of political economy* that the "mode of production in material life determines the general character of the social, political, spiritual processes of life" can thus be said to have closed out a revolution in historiography and social theory which had its beginnings in the eighteenth century.

What is probably most significant about Marx's thought, however, is that he brought together two distinct and previously unrelated concepts that had a far-reaching influence on nineteenth-century historical theorizing. By linking the theory that all history was the history of class struggles with the theory that the conditions of the material environment gave rise to specific institutional and ideological forms, he established a pattern of thought congenial to the nineteenth-century climate of opinion. Whether men were willing to accept his political conclusions or not, few would have denied that he seemed to be moving in the right direction; for it was the century's great hope (as it still is among behavorial scientists) that a coherent, scientifically based, sociological synthesis could be found which would clear away the rubble of uncertainty concerning man and his social relationships. In one way or another the faith that this synthesis could be found, indeed, that it was all but formulated, dominated the thinking of persons as diverse in viewpoint as J. S. Mill, Auguste Comte, and Henry Maine. Lesser men, intellectual journalizers like Leslie Stephen, for one example, gave this confident hope an almost popular currency among the reading classes of the late nineteenth century.

Almost inevitably, however, it was German scholarship that worked most diligently in this direction and sought by massive industry to arrive at a final coherence. For this there were probably two reasons: first, because of the continuing influence of the Hegelian-Marxian intellectual tradition in German academic circles; and, second, because a number of the more influential historical writers, among whom was Werner Sombart, were sympathetic to socialism and almost unconsciously tried to preserve the general outlines of Marxian theory against criticism by broadening its historical scope. It was clear, for example, that if all European history since the end of the middle ages was to be interpreted as a series of class struggles, then Marx's view that the bourgeoisie came into its own during the course of the eighteenth century was simply not comprehensive enough. If the French Revolution marked the emergence of a militant bourgeoisie in France, then what of earlier revolutions? [6] What of the Protestant Reformation, that great sixteenth-century overturn which had ended the sway of the medieval church and its "feudal ideology" in many parts of Europe? Surely these could not be excluded from a theory which claimed universal comprehensiveness in its interpretation of European history? In order to fill the gap there had to be some connection between Protestantism and the capitalist mode of production. Who it was that first remedied this deficiency we cannot be sure. Sombart has been given credit for it, but in the first edition of his *Der moderne Kapitalismus* (Leipzig, 1902) he inferred that the connection was a "well known fact," seemingly proved by the researches of other scholars. There was little doubt in his mind but that Protestantism, particularly in its Calvinist and Quaker varieties, was, according to the established Marxian formula, an ideological manifestation of the economic change brought on by the nascent capitalism of the sixteenth century.[7]

The first serious criticism of this widely circulated assumption came from Wax Weber. In this connection it is well to emphasize that Weber was a critic and not a supporter of Marx's and Sombart's views, for this fact is sometimes forgotten. He rejected the idea that religious ideas were only ideological manifestations of particular social conditions. Ideas for him were, at least in part, autonomous entities with a power to affect social changes. As proof, he cited what seemed to him clear historical evidence that capitalism was a result rather than a cause of the Reformation. He believed that Calvinist theology, in particular, contained certain elements which were peculiarly conducive to rationalized, individualistic economic activity undertaken for profit: not simply for the purpose of enjoying the fruits thereof but rather as a duty, as part, indeed, of a new sense of ethical obligation.[8] Unfortunately, the storm of controversy which followed on the appearance of this suggestion had an effect which Weber could not foresee. By suggesting that the rise of capitalism was influenced by Calvinist

[6] As Marx explained in the *Communist manifesto*, the English revolution of the seventeenth century was a "bourgeois revolution" but an incomplete one which had occurred under "less advanced conditions of civilization."

[7] Werner Sombart, *Der moderne kapitalismus* (Leipzig, 1902), I, 380–81. For various estimates of Sombart's views in this matter see the reviews of his writings contained in *Vierteljahrschrift für Sozial-und Wirtschaftsgeschichte*, XI (1913), 637–40; XIII (1916), 316–19; and XV (1919–21), 111–18.

[8] Cf The Protestant Ethic and the Spirit of Capitalism, Ch. IV.

thought he helped to strengthen the assumption, already strong in some scholarly and intellectual circles, that the two were somehow necessarily and intimately linked together.

In the more than half-century since Weber's hypothesis was first put forward there has scarcely been an end to controversy. Because his view still presupposed an intimate connection between Protestantism or, more specifically, Calvinism and capitalism, some of Weber's critics have overlooked the fact that he was actually trying to reverse the Marxian formula and have gone on to conclude that he was only restating it in a slightly different way. It has even been charged that his theories provided the ammunition for later attacks on Calvinism and other branches of religion by writers who sought to link religious belief with the "unpopularity of Capitalism in the twentieth century." [9] Other opponents, of whom the best known and the friendliest is Tawney, have criticized Weber's views from a totally different position. With impressive scholarship, Tawney argued in the two most famous of his writings on the subject, *The agrarian revolution of the sixteenth century* (London, 1912) and *Religion and the rise of capitalism* (London, 1926), that economic change was ultimately responsible for the transformation of the Christian ethic from the sixteenth century onward. In so doing, he has not gone the whole way and asked us to accept the historiographical stereotype which links the middle classes and Calvinism. What he has attempted to demonstrate is that Calvinism, like most other religious movements stemming from the Reformation, was changed under pressure of economic forces into something that Calvin did not necessarily intend it to become. In so arguing, however, Tawney has taken a position very close to that of Marx while eschewing Marx's original terminology. Moreover, his later writings on the rise of the English gentry during the sixteenth and seventeenth centuries confirm this impression very strongly, since they clearly attempt to account for one of the peculiarities of English history which for long had seemed to put England outside the framework of Marxian theory. He was aware that the country gentlemen and not the merchants had played a decisive role in England's political and social life before the nineteenth century and that the former were to a large extent responsible for the great rebellion against Charles I. By examining various aspects of English social history in the century preceding 1640, he found what seemed to him to be conclusive evidence that the merchants and squires were far more closely linked in terms of interest and out-

[9] H. M. Robertson, *Aspects of the rise of economic individualism* (Cambridge, 1933), p. xi.

look than anyone had previously thought. This linkage, as he saw it, was discernible in the process of economic change which had steadily expanded commercial wealth and made it possible for the merchant to acquire land and, ultimately, the status of a country gentleman. Simultaneously, this expansion transformed the whole body of the English gentry into a class of capitalist entrepreneurs with all the acquisitive habits and economic aspirations peculiar to such a class. As the economic strength of the gentry increased, that of the older established aristocracy declined until the time came when the gentry simply foreclosed the older landowning classes by the violent method of revolution. Thus Tawney was able to explain away the anomalies of the English civil wars that did not fit into the Marxian pattern. Pym, Hampden, Cromwell, all the gentlemen of England who took up arms against the king, became English analogues of the bourgeoisie, and Marx was right after all.

THE WEBER THESIS REEXAMINED *

Winthrop S. Hudson

Weber's initial statement of his thesis was frequently misread, misunderstood, and misinterpreted. Part of the difficulty was a failure to pay sufficient attention to Weber's definition of terms—particularly what he meant by modern capitalism and the spirit of capitalism. Further difficulty was created by those who over-stated the points which Weber was seeking to establish. Even Tawney understood Weber to be asserting that Calvinism, by creating the indispensable psychological climate, was to a very large degree the "parent" of modern capitalism. It is now contended, however, that those who interpreted Weber as saying that modern capitalism was the "offspring" of Calvinism misunderstood him. Weber, it is insisted, never made such a claim and was far too learned and sophisticated to have done so. His intention was much more modest. He was attempting to analyze but one of the many components of the total matrix out of which the

* Reprinted with the permission of the author and the editors of *Church History* (XXX, 1961, 88–99, with omissions).

capitalist spirit emerged. He did no more than suggest that Calvinism engendered a spirit that was congruent with the spirit of capitalism and thus facilitated the development of capitalist society. This brings Weber, of course, largely into agreement with Tawney who said that " 'the capitalist spirit' is as old as history" and that what certain aspects of later Calvinism did was to provide "a tonic which braced its energies and fortified its already vigorous temper."

Whatever Weber may have said or intended, certain general agreements have emerged from the controversy. It is now generally acknowledged that capitalism and the capitalist spirit—even defined as Weber defined these terms—long antedated Calvin's activity at Geneva, that there were other and earlier solvents of those traditional economic attitudes which had served to check the growth of capitalism, and that one of the most significant factors in fostering a capitalist mentality may have been the introduction of double-entry bookkeeping in the fourteenth century. It is further recognized that the teachings of the Schoolmen had inculcated the "economic virtues" and that these moral theologians of the fourteenth and fifteenth centuries had developed a highly rational system of ethics which fostered rational habits of mind and had as its corollary a rational methodizing of life. There is further agreement that Calvinists often constituted a persecuted minority, were frequently forced to migrate, and in many instances were excluded from the professions and public office. Fanfani has pointed out that most minority groups under such circumstances tend to become industrious and frugal and to participate in commercial activities in disproportionate numbers, and consequently such behavior can scarcely be cited as evidence of the influence upon economic developments of the particular faith they professed.[1]

These agreements, however, do not touch Weber's central concern. Believing as he did that the capitalist spirit was an essentially irrational spirit which ran counter to man's natural human instincts, he concluded that only the most powerful of motivations could make it the dominant spirit of a whole culture. "The magical and religious forces, and the ethical ideas of duty based upon them," he noted, "have in the past always been among the most important formative influences upon conduct." Might it not be, he asked himself, that this strange irrational spirit, though now unconnected with any religious interest, once had a religious sanction which gave it meaning and support? He had observed what seemed to him to be a remarkable coinci-

[1] Amintore Fanfani, *Catholicism, Protestantism, and Capitalism* (London, 1935), 160–182.

dence of a particular religious affiliation with a particular social status—specifically, the identification of Calvinism with the industrial and commercial classes of the centers of capitalistic activity—and he concluded that this might offer a clue to the ceaseless drive of the capitalist spirit. He therefore posed the question: Was this coincidence a mere historical accident or was there some inner organic connection between the spread of Calvinism and the rise of modern capitalism?

Weber proceeded on the assumption that the contrast between the economic conservatism of Roman Catholic and Lutheran lands and the strenuous enterprise of Calvinist communities was not an historical accident and that it was Calvinism that had welded the feeble thrust of the aspiring *bourgeoisie* into a disciplined force that was able to transform an entire culture and set its stamp on every aspect of society. The feature of Calvinism which he regarded as of crucial significance in this connection was what seemed to him to be the peculiarly Calvinist concept of "the calling."

The central idea to which Weber appeals in confirmation of his theory is explained in the characteristic phrase "a calling." For Luther, as for most medieval theologians, it had normally meant the state of life in which the individual has been set by Heaven, and against which it was impious to rebel. To the Calvinist, . . . the calling is not a condition in which the individual is born, but a strenuous and exacting enterprise to be chosen by himself, and to be pursued with a sense of religious responsibility.

Labor thereby became not simply an economic means but a spiritual end, and ultimately it became an end in itself. The key to this shift, Weber maintained, was the fact that success in one's calling was interpreted as a sign of God's blessing, and thus evidence of one's election. In commercial life success came to be measured more and more in terms of financial profit, and "the pursuit of riches, which once had been feared as the enemy of religion, was now welcomed as its ally." In the end, this led to an unlimited lust for gain as an end in itself, quite divorced from all moral restraints.

Weber illustrated his thesis with a profuse and wide-ranging selection of examples drawn from history, but he recognized—so Ephraim Fischoff maintains—that his thesis was inadequately documented historically. Weber's approach to the problem, it is asserted, was not historical but sociological. He was utilizing what has been called "a controlled intuitive method"; and what he did—according to his wife—was to create an "ideal-type" on the basis of "careful causal imputation of intuitively apprehended connections" for purposes of sociological analysis. It was not intended to be a final or dogmatic formulation. It was a "tentative effort," a "preliminary investigation," a hypothesis to be checked and validated. But before Weber undertook the research necessary to validate his thesis, he believed that he must first isolate other components in the total matrix and define them in terms of "ideal types." Then at the end of the process of intuitive analysis, it would be both possible and necessary to return to the historical question "to determine how closely the empirical phenomena approached the ideal types he had formulated." [2]

Weber never found time to undertake the historical task of validating his thesis by a detailed study of the actual religious and economic history of specific communities. Thus, from an historian's point of view, he left himself open to the quite valid charge that he sought to demonstrate, for example, the effect of Calvinism on the economic life of Holland and the Rhineland by utilizing illustrations drawn from Anglo-Saxon writers. It has also been suggested—somewhat facetiously, to be sure—that he raised the question whether or not John Calvin was a Calvinist, for he defined Calvinism largely in terms of the points of view represented by John Wesley and Benjamin Franklin. Furthermore, it has been acknowledged that Weber on occasion fell victim to the temptation to manipulate history in the interest of his thesis. Such manipulation, says Tawney, is always "the temptation of one who expounds a new and fruitful idea" and Weber's essay is "not altogether free" of this defect.

Subsequent research has demonstrated several things with reference to the Weber thesis. First of all, it has been demonstrated that the correlation between the spread of Calvinism and the development of a vigorous capitalist economy was not as uniform as he had supposed. Presbyterian Scotland, for example, witnessed no great surge of economic activity, whereas Roman Catholic Flanders did. Hungary actually declined economically during the most flourishing period of Calvinist activity. Some of the conclusions that have been reached by economic historians as a result of their research have been summarized by Fischoff as follows:

On the basis of investigations into the history of Holland—and it must be recalled that this republic was probably the first country in which capitalism developed on a large scale—recent Netherlands historians like DeJong, Knappert and de Pater find no proof to sustain such a theory of the con-

[2] Ephraim Fischoff, "The Protestant Ethic and the Spirit of Capitalism: the History of a Controversy," *Social Research*, XI (1944); reprinted in Robert W. Green, *Protestantism and Capitalism*.

nection between Calvinism and capitalism among the Netherlanders. Further, Beins' researches into the economic ethic of the Calvinist church in the Netherlands between 1565 and 1650 lead him to raise serious objections to Weber's thesis. A similar view is expressed in the important economic history of the Netherlands by Baasch, who stresses the secular factors in the evolution of capitalism in Holland which made the Netherlanders the chief bankers of the seventeenth century and by the end of the eighteenth made the colony of Jews in Amsterdam the largest in Europe. The same adverse conclusion is reached by Koch's investigation of the economic development of the lower Rhine area and Andrew Sayous' study of the Genevans; Hashagen's essay on the relation between Calvinism and capitalism in the German Rhineland comes to similar conclusions. Evidence has also accumulated that Calvinism did not have any necessary effect on the rise of capitalism in Hungary, Scotland or France.

These findings, of course, do not disprove Weber's thesis, for there were many factors involved in each specific situation, but they do raise serious questions and they cannot be construed as providing support for it.

In the second place, Weber's assumption that for his purposes "ascetic Protestantism" could be treated "as a single whole" has been shown to be false. It has been made abundantly clear, as Tawney has acknowledged, that the economic individualism which Weber identified in certain aspects of late post-Restoration Puritanism would have "horrified" the earlier Calvinists, including the English Puritans. "No contrast could be more violent," says Tawney, "than that between the iron collectivism, the almost military discipline, the remorseless and violent rigors practiced in Calvin's Geneva, and preached elsewhere, if in a milder form, by his disciples, and the impatient rejection of all traditional restrictions on economic enterprise which was the temper of the English business world after the Civil War." To suggest to "the Puritan of any period in the century between the accession of Elizabeth and the Civil War" that he was a friend of "economic or social license" would have seemed "wildly inappropriate" both to him and to his critics who accused him of being intolerably meticulous. Even Troeltsch admits that a kind of "Christian Socialism" was "contained, from the very outset, in the Genevan ideal of the Holy Community" and that it was continued in the various Calvinist communities "under the cross."

The significant question to Tawney is the question as to how the change came about that permitted the free play of the acquisitive spirit within a movement which hitherto had been anti-Mammon in orientation and anti-individualistic in temper. The explanation for such a radical shift, Tawney believed, was not to be found simply in the impact of economic change upon Calvinist thinking. It stemmed, he asserted, from "the very soul of Calvinism" itself.

In reality, the same ingredients were present throughout, but they were mixed in changing proportions, and exposed to different temperatures at different times. Like traits of individual character which are suppressed till the approach of maturity releases them, the tendencies in Puritanism, which were to make it later a potent ally of the movement against the control of economic relations in the name either of social morality or of the public interest, did not reveal themselves till political and economic changes had prepared a congenial environment for their growth.

Like Weber, Tawney found the key to the separation of economic from ethical interests in what they both considered "the very heart of Puritan theology"—the Calvinist conception of the "calling." Applied to commercial life, it meant that "poverty . . . was not a misfortune to be pitied and relieved, but a moral failing to be condemned," and that riches were "the blessing which rewards the triumph of energy and will." "By a kind of happy preestablished harmony . . . , success in business is in itself almost a sign of spiritual grace, for it is proof that a man has labored faithfully in his vocation, and that 'God has blessed his trade.' " The doctrine of the calling was thus the bridge by which, over the course of time, ethical distinctions in commercial life were obliterated and the service of Mammon was identified with service to God.

If more recent research has demonstrated that the correlation of the spread of Calvinism to the development of capitalism was not as uniform as had been supposed and that for its first century and a half Calvinism was far from friendly to economic licence, it is now clear that the Calvinist doctrine of the calling has also been misunderstood and misinterpreted. First of all, Robertson disposed of the philological argument which attempted to portray the concept as something utterly new and unique, and Fanfani acknowledged that "the idea of vocation, attributed by Weber to the Protestants, was a living idea before the Reformation, and remained alive in the Catholic camp even after." In the second place, it has been made abundantly evident that the concept of a Christian's calling was not an invitation to amass riches but rather it served as a bridle to restrain avarice and ambition. The constant emphasis was upon the danger of riches and the Christian's duty to avoid striving after them. It was precisely the conviction that one's calling was God's gift for which, as a good steward, the Christian must render an accounting that served as a check to covetousness. Far from being a means to accumulate financial gain, one's calling was the normal channel through which love of neighbor was to be expressed and his welfare sought. The Dutch Calvinists were typical in regarding action born of desire for gain as a sign of madness, and in asserting that, while normally one should be digilent in his daily work, excessive labor is to be condemned as robbing time and energy from the many duties that are involved in the service of God. In the same way, nothing is more characteristic of Richard Baxter—the most conspicuous figure of post-Restoration Puritanism—than his intensely anti-Mammon temper. He constantly insisted that God and Mammon were antithetical, and he lashed out at the hypocrisy of those who thought that they could be reconciled.

Among Baxter's contemporaries in late seventeenth century England, there were those, to be sure, who did interpret financial success in one's calling as an indication of divine approval. It should be noted, however, that this transformation of the concept of the calling from a bridle to avarice and ambition into a comfortable doctrine congenial to an uninhibited commercial spirit represented a one hundred and eighty degree shift in interpretation. How are we to account for so marked a change? Certainly, we cannot attribute it to the Calvinist conception of the calling when it was the conception of the calling itself that underwent change. It is quite inconceivable that the Calvinist conception of the calling, as it was understood for almost a century and a half, could have bred a spirit of capitalism, but it is conceivable that the spirit of capitalism could have gradually modified and in the end completely transformed the Calvinist conception of the calling. And when it was so transformed, it could no longer—in any proper use of terms—be regarded as Calvinistic.

The clue to what occurred is provided by Fanfani in his book *Catholicism, Protestantism, and Capitalism.* Fanfani acknowledges that there were, both before and after the Reformation, many Catholics who "acted in a capitalistic manner" and "introduced a capitalistic mode of life among their Catholic contemporaries." It would be easy to arrive at the conclusion that capitalism was the "offspring" of Catholicism since "capitalism was born in a Europe that was still wholly Catholic" and "Catholics indisputably fostered its growth." But Fanfani rightly notes that those Catholics who did act in a capitalistic manner were not "acting in conformity with Catholic social ethics."

Thus the influence they exerted was not because they were Catholics but in spite of their being Catholics.

Max Weber, Fanfani pointed out, had set for himself a false problem. Weber had assumed that somehow men need to be "called" to devote themselves to riches. "A man does not 'by nature,'" Weber had said, "wish to earn more and more money, but simply to live as he is accustomed to live and to earn as much as is necessary for that purpose." Troeltsch also had suggested that the seeking of profit as an end in itself was in "opposition to natural human instincts," although he admitted that there always have been "unscrupulous individuals who are simply out for gain" and who have on occasion "interrupted" the natural order. Such individuals, however, are out of line with "ordinary human instincts." Tawney, to be sure, had acknowledged that the "'capitalist spirit' is as old as history." But he did not base his analysis upon this assumption. "The emergence of the idea that 'business is business' . . . ," he insisted, "did not win so painless a triumph as is sometimes suggested." It necessitated a real *tour de force,* for Tawney also believed that basically greed, enterprise, and competition were departures from the "natural state of things." Such an assumption, Fanfani asserted, represents a misreading of human nature. As "against Weber," he said, "we would point out that man has an inborn instinct for gain" and "that external factors either check this instinct or encourage it." How does one explain the establishment of a capitalist spirit in Roman Catholic lands? There were many forces that served to encourage the development of such a spirit, but the major factor which made possible its establishment, Fanfani asserted, was "the waning of faith"—a faith which hitherto had served as a check to the acquisitive spirit.

With the weakening of faith remorse becomes rare; the 'is' is no longer compared with the "should-be," and that which "is" is accepted and exploited in accordance with its own standards. . . .
All the circumstances that, in the Middle Ages, led to a waning of faith explain the progressive establishment of the capitalistic spirit, for the precapitalist spirit rests on facts that are not seen, but must be held by faith. Those faithful to it sacrifice a certain result for a result that is guaranteed by faith; they eschew a certain mode of action in the certainty of losing riches, but believing that they will gain a future reward in heaven. Let man lose this belief, and nothing remains for him, rationally speaking, but to act in a capitalistic manner.

In reply to Weber, Fanfani would insist that, since the capitalist spirit does not run counter to man's natural human instincts, it is not necessary to posit some strange powerful irrational motivation in order to explain how it could become the dominant spirit of an entire culture.

But what, it may be asked, is the explanation of the "halo of sanctification" that was cast about the "convenient vices" of the business man? Is not the concept of the calling needed to explain this phenomenon? It would seem strange to one who is at all familiar with the Biblical record that this should be considered a problem that needs explanation. The Biblical writings provide abundant illustrations of man's perennial endeavor to hide the nakedness of his self-interest behind a cloak of religious pretensions. Again and again in the Scriptures, we read how men attempted to console themselves with the comfortable assurance that worldly prosperity was an indication of divine favor; and again and again, we find that beguiling assurance exposed as empty and hollow. At this point also the Weber thesis would seem to have posed a false problem as a result of misreading the human story.

But what then is to be said of the undoubted coincidence of Calvinism and vigorous economic life in certain centers of western Europe? This is probably to be explained largely in terms of historical accident. "The main explanation," says Fanfani, "must lie with circumstances extraneous to the religious phenomenon." Calvinism took root on the Atlantic frontier of western Europe at a time when trade, for a variety of reasons, was shifting from the East to the West. It also took place at a time when technical developments had made possible a more complex and large-scale economic life, and at a time when France was beset by internal strife, Spain was in manifest decline, and England and Holland were beginning to enjoy a practical or legal monopoly in most non-European markets.

Calvinism, of course, did inculcate the economic virtues of industry, frugality, honesty, prudence, and sobriety, and this fact is not without significance. Furthermore, Calvinism inculcated these virtues the more effectively because the movement was at the peak of its religious intensity and passion. Given these qualities in the particular situation in which Calvinists found themselves, it was inevitable that they should prosper. And given their particular setting in the commercial centers and their growing prosperity, it is obvious that they occupied a particularly exposed position of peril so far as the integrity of their faith was concerned. Thus their basic convictions were much more subject to the attrition of the world than would have otherwise been true. Moreover, there is always an ebb and flow in tides of spiritual life, and the peculiar circumstances of these particular communities, once the early heroic age of Calvinism was past, contributed to the ebb. The waning of faith then facilitated an adjustment to the claims of commercial enterprise and this resulted in a transformation of the whole mood and temper of these Calvinist groups.

The chief factor in the triumph of the spirit of capitalism would seem to be this: when the faith, which hitherto had served as a check to the acquisitive spirit, became more and more nominal, the adherents of that faith refused to be bound any longer by what they considered to be the antiquated rules imposed by that faith. In other words, a rising class of self-made men found the attraction of a free world of business much greater than that of a waning religious ideal. "Their demand," says Tawney, "was the one which is usual in such circumstances. It was that business affairs should be left to be settled by business men, unhampered by the intrusions of an antiquated morality, or by misconceived arguments of public policy." A perfect illustration of the adjustment they required is to be found in the publication of *The New Whole Duty of Man, containing the Faith as well as Practice of a Christian: Made Easy for the Practice of the Present Age* (1744). It was published to replace the first *Whole Duty of Man* (1658), because the earlier volume was not "by any means suited to the present times; for how can it be? it having been written near one hundred years since." What was needed was what the subtitle indicated—a conception of duty "made easy for the practice of the present age."

The desired separation of economic activity from ethical restraint, however, was not accomplished without a struggle. As Tawney has observed:

Even in the very capital of European commerce and finance, an embittered controversy was occasioned by the refusal to admit usurers to communion or to confer degrees upon them; it was only after a storm of pamphleteering, in which the theological faculty of the University of Utrecht performed prodigies of zeal and ingenuity, that the States of Holland and West Friesland closed the agitation by declaring that the Church had no concern with questions of banking. In the French Calvinist churches, the decline of discipline had caused lamentations a generation earlier. In America, the theocracy of Massachusetts, merciless alike to religious liberty and to economic license, was about to be undermined by the rise of new States like Rhode Island and Pennsylvania, whose tolerant, individualist and utilitarian temper was destined to find its greatest representative in the golden common sense of Benjamin Franklin. 'The sin of our too great fondness for trade, to the neglecting of our more valuable interests,' wrote a Scottish divine in 1709, when Glasgow was on the eve of a triumphant outburst of commercial enterprise, 'I humbly think will be written upon our judgment. . . . I am sure the Lord is remarkably frowning upon our trade . . . since it was put in the room of religion.'

What Tawney is actually saying here is that Calvinism, far from fostering and strengthening and reinforcing the spirit of capitalism, was itself suffering defeat as a prelude to being reshaped and altered and transformed by the development of the busy commercial spirit which it sought to restrain. What the record makes clear is that the Calvinist churches lost the power before they lost the will "to bind business within the discipline of Christian justice and charity."

The "loss of power" to place an effective restraint upon the temptations of avarice and ambition in commercial life is simply another way of saying that there was a breakdown of ecclesiastical discipline. Such a breakdown always occurs when there is a "waning of faith" in the community at large, but there may have been other factors which contributed to it and made Protestantism particularly susceptible to the crumbling of ecclesiastical authority.

Fanfani has suggested that fostering of religious toleration by Protestantism was one of these factors. Many Protestants, he notes, were forced into exile, being "persecuted in their own countries" and "viewed with suspicion in their new ones," and "as a result of their misfortunes" became "fervent apostles of religious toleration and freedom—a fact of immense importance for the expansion of business, and highly prized by the capitalist."

It is indisputable that Protestantism, by immigration and otherwise, destroyed the unity of the State in the religious sphere and made its restoration impossible, so that King and subjects were faced with the problem of shelving the religious question in order to obtain such unity. Protestantism thus obliged the States to face the problem of freedom of conscience, which, advocated by authoritative Protestants, once solved, meant the removal of an obstacle to economic life and encouraged the tendency to count the religious question among the problems that could be left out of reckoning.

The role of religious toleration in the breakdown of ecclesiastical discipline is a much more complicated and debatable matter than Fanfani's discussion of it would make it appear, but this much is true: it did force religious bodies to rely upon the power of persuasion rather than upon legal coercion to maintain their influence in society.

There are two factors—one theological and one ecclesiastical—which may have been of greater importance in the assimilation of much of Protestantism to the model of the world. Theologically, Protestantism on the basis of its central affirmation can never make a claim to any unambiguous or infallible apprehension of divine truth, and thus it is more open to new currents of thought than would otherwise be true. Ecclesiastically, by largely destroying the distinction between clergy and laity, it placed its destiny to a very large degree in the hands of the whole body of the faithful rather than in a clerical caste which could more easily be subjected to discipline. Furthermore, this emphasis upon the priesthood of all believers tended in many Protestant denominations —whatever their ostensible polity—toward an exaggerated congregationalism which emphasized the autonomy of the local congregation and cancelled out the restraints which a larger ecclesiastical jurisdiction theoretically could maintain. This is a problem which has been inadequately investigated and which certainly demands urgent attention. It is not immediately apparent, however, that religious bodies with tightly-knit ecclesiastical control have always escaped accommodation to the spirit of the world. It would still seem to be true, therefore, that "the waning of faith" remains as the chief explanation of the relationship of religion to the rise of an uninhibited capitalist spirit in western society.

BIBLIOGRAPHY

A. Biéler, La pensée économique et sociale de Calvin (Geneva: 1959). Robert W. Green (ed.), Protestantism and Capitalism. The Weber Thesis and Its Critics (Boston: 1959). Harold J. Grimm, "Social Forces in the German Reformation," Church History, XXXI (1962), 3–13. Karl Holl, The Cultural Significance of the Reformation (New York: 1959). Herbert Lüthy, "Nochmals: Calvinismus und Kapitalismus! Über die Irrwege einer sozialhistorischen Diskussions," Schweizerische Zeitschrift für Geschichte, No. 2 (1961), 129–156. Kurt Samuelsson, Religion and Economic Action (London: 1961). [The Editor.]

THE ORIGINS OF PURITANISM *

Leonard J. Trinterud

One of the commonly accepted views of English and American Puritanism is that its theology derived directly from the writings of John Calvin. Since Calvin is usually thought of as a rather rigid pre-

* Reprinted with permission of the author and the editors of Church History (XX, 1951, 37–57, with omissions).

destinarian who believed that God was all and man was nought in the scheme of salvation, it is also a common belief among many historians that Puritanism was an equally inflexible system of theological determinism. Both interpretations are now seriously questioned by scholars who presently agree that neither Calvinism nor Puritanism was quite so inflexibly deterministic as was once thought. In the following selection Professor Trinterud points out that the theological sources of Puritanism were not solely Calvinistic nor completely predestinarian. As a consequence, Puritanism developed a body of beliefs which belie its historic caricature as a dogmatic predestinarian system of theology.

It has been the peculiar lot of Puritanism that, while most men will agree that its influence—good or evil—upon Anglo-Saxon culture and history has been profound, yet great disagreement exists as to just what Puritanism was, how it began, and what aspects of traditional Anglo-Saxon thought and life are traceable to Puritanism. The most common view is that Puritanism was imported into England from Calvinistic Geneva by the returning Marian exiles. This view must then go on to account for the many non-Calvinistic elements in the Puritanism of the Civil War era. Another school of thought has sought to identify Puritanism with the beginnings of democratic political, social and economic ideals during the Tudor-Stuart era. Almost diametrically opposed to this is yet another school of thought which finds in Puritanism an ultra-rightist authoritarianism in theology and politics, and the seed-bed of an unbridled and pharisaical capitalism. Still others see in Puritanism the long hard travail which gave birth to the ideal of complete freedom for the individual in all phases of life. Of necessity, each of these interpretations, and others not here mentioned, has sought to ground itself in the history of the English Reformation, and so we have many quite different accounts of the origins and history of Puritanism.

The most obvious excuse for attempting another account of the origins and genius of Puritanism would be that the present disagreements cannot be final. However, a far better reason lies in the fact that Puritan studies made in recent years by scholars in England, America, and Europe, covering almost every conceivable phase of English life in the sixteenth and seventeenth centuries, provide us with a vast body of new data in the light of which the older data and interpretations are being critically re-examined. What seems to be emerging is an account of Puritanism in which the heritage from medieval English thought and life is the controlling element. Puritanism was indigenous, not exotic, to England. Moreover, these foreign influences which were taken up by the English Puritans as they sought to give intellectual form to their ideas and ideals, were taken up not primarily from John Calvin of Geneva, but from the Reformers of the Rhineland: Zwingli, Jud, Bullinger, Oecolampadius, Capito, Bucer, Martyr, and a host of other leaders in the Reformation movement in Zurich, Basel, Strassburg, and other Rhineland cities. The Genevan influences came late, after the essential patterns of Puritanism had been established. Furthermore, political, theological, and ecclesiastical considerations combined to defeat the bid for power which was made by the small, but able, group who sponsored these Genevan views.

Puritanism emerged in Tudor England in the thought and work of men such as William Tyndale, John Frith, John Bale, John Hooper, John Bradford, and their associates. By these men a pattern was set which enjoyed a steady and unbroken course of development until it came to expression in the Long Parliament, the Civil Wars, the Westminster Assembly of Divines, the Commonwealth, and the Protectorate. Puritanism embraced such divergent religious alignments as the moderate Episcopalians, the Presbyterians, the Independents, and the Particular Baptists. Politically Puritanism embraced advocates of a limited monarchy, of responsible parliamentary government, of unlimited rule by parliament, and of recurrent revolution. Despite this wide range of conflicting views, the basic pattern of them all was set before the Marian Exile. What the advocates of these many ideas had in common made it possible for them to unite in revolution. But, the divergent lines of development which each group had taken since their common beginnings made it impossible for them to unite in creating a Puritan regime in England. Their ideas, however, remained as a permanent leaven in English thought and life because they were authentic expressions of the English spirit and heritage.

The problem which any reforming or revolutionary group must always face is that of authority. An authority must be found which can be offered to men as having greater right than the authority of the status quo. Yet, while this new authority must have enough popular appeal that it will lead men to reject, even at great cost, the older authority, it must also be such that it will command the obedience of the rebels to itself and make possible a new, or reformed society. When the Roman Catholic authority was rejected by the Reformers little indeed was left standing. Not merely matters of religious opinion had to be re-stated, but a new basis had to be found for personal and public religious life and morals, educations, civil government, family life, and even international relations. In the Rhineland, an area in which more

liberal views of freedom and liberty had long been prevalent, recourse
had often been had by many political thinkers to the idea of authority
grounded in natural law and social contract. So also the religious reformers of the Rhineland had recourse to an authority grounded in the
divine law and a covenant between God and man. It was definitive
for Puritanism that a similar religious authority had been advocated
widely by several English reformers before the death of Henry VIII.
Under Edward VI it became virtually standard for English theology.
Politically, the natural law-social contract theory had had some vogue
in medieval English thought, but it came into open alliance with religious reform first in John Ponet, John Knox, and Christopher Goodman during the Marian Exile.

The origins of the state-compact, or social contract, theory in politics
need not here be re-stated. It is enough to note that by the late Medieval
Era the state contract idea was being used by the Conciliarists in their
struggle against the claims of the papacy, and by the more liberal political thinkers of the day. The framework of the idea was that natural
law, prior to all authority and all positive law, existed in the reason of
all men. On the basis of this natural law, which was thought to guarantee the binding character of all agreements, society had been first constituted by contract between God on the one hand and the people and
the king on the other hand. Subsequent to this general social contract
a particular contract had been entered into between the king and the
people whereby each party bound itself to a particular form of government in which their common obligation to serve God could be actu-
alized in their history. Thus the authority of the king was presumably
limited by natural law and by the state contract with his subjects.
Moreover, the obligations of the subjects were not based directly upon
natural law, but upon the supposed contract—hence the king was truly
the ruler.

On the religious side a somewhat analogous covenant theory had
been slowly building up all through Christian history. The idea of a
covenant between God and man was an important aspect of Biblical
thought. So also in the early Church the idea of a natural law given
in man's reason at his creation appeared very early and was attached
to the Biblical idea of covenant by Athanasius. The idea was, however,
never exploited further, it seems. Augustine used the idea of state-
contract in political theory and no doubt this influenced some religious
speculation along similar lines. Nicholas de Lyra utilized the idea of
"treaty of reconciliation" (pactum = pax factum) as the statement of
the manner in which salvation took place. So also papal apologists fre-

quently utilized the notion that baptism was the equivalent of a contract to serve God, hence when kings accepted Christian baptism they in effect made a contract with God's vicar, the pope. This idea was utilized even by Bellarmine. Frequently in this medieval development of the state contract theory the notion of "juristic persons," or "juristic corporations," or personified states or groups arises. Usually these notions carry with them the idea of representation, or representative personalities which act on behalf of all.

As the theological concept of the covenant arose among the Rhineland reformers, it utilized most of the ideas found in the medieval contract theories. Natural law was closely related to man's reason, and both were supposed to have been possessed unimpaired by Adam prior to the fall. However, the idea of a covenant at creation does not occur in the Bible, hence the earlier covenant theories are actually based upon the notion of a covenant of redemption between God and Abraham in which Abraham's part is often close to that assigned by political thinkers to a "juristic person." The Bible, indeed, mentions also a covenant with Noah, and even in the earliest stages of the covenant theology this covenant is noted. Also, the so-called *proto-evangelium,* or promise of salvation made to Adam and Eve after the fall is called a covenant. But, since these two covenants raised the gravest of problems in theology—namely the problem of election *versus* universalism—the covenant theologians until about 1580 built their whole theology upon the covenant with Abraham. When one examines their very few extra-Biblical authorities for their covenant notion, they cite Jewish targums and classical writers most frequently. For the most part they assume the covenant theory as something everywhere patent in the Bible.

While the covenant theology made some headway, therefore, during the era of Henry VIII, it was during the brief, but exceedingly important reign of Edward VI that the covenant scheme became fixed in English theology. During Edward's reign there came to England a number of famous Rhineland leaders, Peter Martyr, Bucer, Tremellius (a converted Jewish Hebraist of great ability), Fagius, Dryander, and others. These men, together with the literary influence of their continental friends who were also covenant theologians, set the stamp of international Reformed approval, so to speak, upon this theology. . . .

The Marian Exile was decisive for the English reformation in many ways. It brought numerous leading ministers, and a goodly number of theological students out of England into the Rhineland cities. These exiles were not all of one mind on many topics. Their troubles among themselves, and their troubles with the homeland produced a number of vigorous debates, and several important publications. Bishop John Ponet issued his *Shorte Treatise of Politike Pouuer* . . . which set forth in vigorous fashion the state-contract theory. John Knox and Christopher Goodman followed shortly with their even more vigorous statements of the same idea.

In Geneva William Whittingham, Anthony Gilby, and others, issued a new translation of the Bible into English which was equipped with an elaborate set of prefaces and footnotes. This apparatus followed the pattern set already by John Calvin, namely, the use of the state-contract theory in political matters coupled with a very different view of the covenant in matters theological. For Calvin, and so in the Geneva Bible, the covenant of God is God's promise to man, which obligates God to fulfill. Moreover, in the incarnation, death and resurrection of Christ God did actually fulfill that promise to which his covenant bound him. Therefore, the sacraments are witnesses, attestations, or seals to the effect that God has long since fulfilled his covenant, his promise. Therefore, covenant and testament are identical. In the covenant theory of the Rhineland and of the English reformers the covenant is a conditional promise on God's part, which has the effect of drawing out of man a responding promise of obedience, thus creating a mutual pact or treaty. The burden of fulfillment rests upon man, for he must first obey in order to bring God's reciprocal obligation into force. Theologically, of course, the difference between these two views is of the greatest moment.

The very necessities within which the Marian Exiles found themselves required that they organize themselves into congregations or churches while away from England. Here the medieval notion that all bodies politic come first into being by a contract provided pattern enough for them. Moreover, their political activities are clear indications of the fact that they were actually alive to the pertinence of the state contract theory. Little other strictly theological literature was issued by the exiles. The Genevan party of the exile was a minority group in all ways. The majority group was settled in the German Rhineland.

Upon the death of Queen Mary the Genevan group made a bid for leadership among all the exiles on the basis of a set of strong demands which were to be presented to Queen Elizabeth by the entire group. The bid failed, and in a very short time the control of the English Church was in the hands of the non-Genevan party of the exiles, and not one of the Genevan party ever gained an important role in the Elizabethan English Church. The political activities of the Genevan group, and their liturgical views are generally cited as being responsible for their failure to gain any leading part under Elizabeth's "settlement" of religious affairs.

The name "Puritan" first emerged during the vestiarian controversy which began in 1559 and continued until about 1567. During these years the more radical group of English reformers sought to go beyond Elizabeth's compromise between Roman and Evangelical views, and to bring in a more drastic reformation movement. While these radicals did, indeed, wish to root out these things in liturgical practice which they considered as "Romish," nevertheless this move was intended as merely the beginning of the desired more drastic reformation. No one saw this more clearly than Elizabeth and the bishops. Hence Elizabeth refused to grant any consideration to the radicals, and drove the reluctant bishops into the fray. Some of the bishops refused utterly, others temporized, and some became ardent supporters of the Queen's unlimited authority as Supreme Governor of the Church in England. The issue throughout the controversy remained, however, this, wherein lay authority within the Church in England?

The next challenge to Elizabeth's authority was much better grounded, and much better organized. In 1572 an "Admonition" was presented to Parliament asking that certain structural, liturgical and doctrinal reforms be legislated for the Church by Parliament. This move struck hard in two directions. It assumed that Parliament had full authority to make these changes. The argument was that since Parliament had instituted the settlement of religious affairs upon which Elizabeth was then acting, it also had power to alter this settlement. In the second place it called for an organization of the Church upon the basis of a series of representative church courts elected by the people. Such a system would make impossible any control of the Church by Elizabeth or the bishops. This two-pronged attack, led by John Field, Thomas Wilcox, Thomas Cartwright, and others compelled Elizabeth and her two leading bishops, John Whitgift and Richard Bancroft, to exert their most strenuous efforts in order to make an effective opposition. The Court of High Commission, the *ex officio* oath, the Star Chamber, and the episcopal powers of imprisonment without trial, eventually drove this "Presbyterian" movement, as it came to be called, underground.

Far-reaching consequences came of the struggle, however. Bancroft and Richard Hooker were moved to write classic statements of episcopal theory—Bancroft's was based upon divine-right and apostolic succession, and Hooker's on reason, tradition and state contract. Moreover,

Cartwright was moved to do that which no previous advocate of church government by elected, representative church courts had done, namely assert a divine right for this so-called Presbyterian system. Calvin had never made this claim, nor had any other Continental Reformed theologian.

Two theories of church and state were now in conflict in England. Both agreed that church and state were not two entities, but rather the one people under two aspects of one sovereignty. To the episcopal party led by Whitgift and Bancroft, the queen ruled supremely in England by divine right through two arms or regiments, church and state. To the presbyterian party Parliament was supreme in England as the juristic corporation, or representative body, empowered by the social contract to rule in England as the representatives of the people, through two arms or regiments, church and state. The contract theory of government always involved a dualism of ruler and people. The presbyterian party did not look upon Parliament as the ruler but as the juristic person which was the people. They were, therefore, not anti-monarchical, but desired only to restrain the power of the throne by means of the contract notion.

A further development also now took place. In much of Europe the political struggle against the divine right of kings had been going on during the second half of the sixteenth century. In all of these struggles the natural law-social contract notion had played the central role. Nearly all of these political theorists were allied with some Reformed Church, whether of the Rhineland, of France, or of French-speaking Switzerland. As these men, and their theologian colleagues, sought to weave together one complete theological-political-social theory the older theological doctrine of the covenant could not be used, for it was a covenant of redemption restricted entirely to the elect. Increasing mention is found during these years of a "covenant of creation," a "covenant of nature," and similar ideas. But, it was not until about 1580 that a wholly systematic re-organization of the covenant theology emerged.

At Heidelberg University two Reformed theologians, Zachary Ursinus and Caspar Olevianus, who had been deeply committed to the covenant theology for years, seem to have been the architects of the final formulation of the covenant scheme. By the 1580s the idea of a "covenant of works," so-called, made between God and Adam, who represented all mankind, had begun to have considerable vogue on the Continent. This covenant of works provided a theological basis for a moral, civil, and religious obligation binding upon all men, elect or non-elect, regenerate or unregenerate, professedly Christian or pagan.

Into this covenant of works the whole state contract theory was incorporated by the theologians. The natural law of the state contract was also the natural law of the covenant of works. On the Continent the practical applications of this new covenant scheme were never very fully exploited. Puritanism, however, was anything but blind to the possibilities which were inherent in this new scheme.

In 1585 Dudley Fenner, an associate of Cartwright, in his exile in Holland, published a most thoroughly worked out covenant scheme utilizing the double covenant idea, a covenant of works, and a covenant of grace or redemption. Cartwright had adopted the idea himself, and very quickly the ·Puritan group began to utilize the double-covenant scheme as something generally received by all. Moreover, as the Puritan religious movement and the parliamentary political movement began to make common cause they had also now a common theoretical scheme. Parliamentary thought on the state contract had had a long history in England reaching back as far as John Fortescue in the 15th century. By 1590 the double-covenant scheme was being used also by some Scottish theologians.

During these same years, the 1580s, among those who no longer hoped for reform of the Church in England, the idea of the church covenant took on greater significance. In political theory society came into being only by a contract. Theoretically, therefore, the possibility of reverting to a state of nature could be posited. This was, of course, revolution, and might or might not involve tyrannicide. The old authorities all ceased to be binding, and men were free to contract anew on whatever basis they chose. As small religious groups began to withdraw from the Church in England, going either into exile abroad, or underground in England, they claimed the right to "gather" themselves into churches by means of a "church covenant." The history of these Separatist groups has been well worked out and need not here be re-traced. It is enough to note this its theoretical basis: Some of these radical Separatist groups rejected all ideas of predestination, and carried their church covenant to the extent of receiving theologically nothing beyond that which was accepted by the mutual agreement of the brethren. This idea of reverting to nature by revolution, and reconstituting solely by mutual agreement, lacked one essential element of the older contract scheme, namely its dualism. Once the idea of the king in politics, or the creed, the order, or the liturgy in theology, had been eliminated there was no longer any "given" or "established" form or norm in society. Recurrent, or even perpetual, revolution was possible, for mutual agreement of the majority of the people provided no check upon the number of times that the people might change their minds in politics, in doctrine, in order, or in liturgy.

Yet another group also arose among the Puritans, namely the Independents. This group were theologically very rigidly orthodox, with a strong sense of norm in theology. Yet in church order and liturgy they believed in the idea of covenant, or even of mutual agreement. Many of them, however, rejected all idea of revolution politically and theologically, and desired only adjustments within the existing structure. Politically they desired a limited monarchy and a strengthened parliament. Theologically they wished at first no more than the right to exist within the Church in England as conscientious non-conformists until such a time as the Church might have become more fully reformed.

During the first decades of the seventeenth century the covenant theology was received in greater or lesser degree by many sorts of men. Launcelot Andrews, Archbishop James Usher, John Lightfoot, and numerous moderate episcopalians were adherents of this scheme. Among the Presbyterian and Independent Puritans scarcely a single important figure was not a covenant theologian, or federalist. Among the Particular Baptists many were federalists, while the radical idea of mutual agreement was found among the General Baptists and radical Separatists. As early as 1572 Cartwright had noted that disinterest in the Geneva Bible was growing. A federalist Puritan, John Reynolds, at the Hampden Court conference had urged the preparation of a new translation of the Bible, and the edition of 1611 had been due to his suggestion. Although numerous editions of Calvin's works had been issued during the Elizabethan era, it is significant that from 1603 to 1700 only eight printings of any and all of Calvin's works were made in England and Scotland combined. Moreover, even before the Civil War well-known Puritans were cool toward, and quite independent of, Calvin's theology. The covenant theology had won its brief struggle for supremacy with the Geneva Bible and Calvin's theology.

Though the initial impulses toward both the early and the final forms of the covenant theology seem to have come to English reformers from the Rhineland, nevertheless this does not indicate that this entire body of religious thinking and living was not truly and indigenously English. The covenant or federal theology was only an intellectual formulation into which the older English piety, practice and preaching was fitted. Moreover, this covenant scheme had its great appeal in that it could so readily and simply give intellectual expression to the Augustinian theology, the lush, warm flow of mystical piety and devotion, the bride-mysticism, the rich, highly involved allegorical interpretation of the Bible, especially the Song of Songs, the preaching of penitence, the love of pilgrimages and the pilgrim motif, all of which had since medieval times played so great a role in English religious life, and all of which was quite specifically English. The Puritan preachers wove all these themes and *motifs* into the covenant scheme, and portrayed them in moving and dramatic sermons. That which was borrowed from the Rhineland was not a view of the Christian life, but a preacher's tool or vehicle. The Puritan remained in all essentials an English Christian.

BIBLIOGRAPHY

Everett Emerson, "Calvin and Covenant Theology," *Church History*, XXV (1956), 136–144. William Haller, *The Rise of Puritanism* (New York: 1939); *Liberty and Reformation in the Puritan Revolution* (New York: 1955). Marshall M. Knappen, *Tudor Puritanism* (Chicago: 1939). Perry Miller, "The Marrow of Puritan Divinity," *Publications of the Colonial Society of Massachusetts*, XXII (1937); *The New England Mind;* Vol. I: *The Seventeenth Century* (New York: 1939). Alan Simpson, *Puritanism in Old and New England* (Chicago: 1955). [The Editor.]

PURITAN RADICALISM AND THE ENLIGHTENMENT *

George L. Mosse

Traditionally, historians think of the eighteenth century as marking a sharp change in religious outlook from that of the seventeenth century. The eighteenth century is usually regarded as secular in point of view and the seventeenth as still deeply imbued with the long-standing religious outlook of Christianity, in spite of the denominational conflicts caused by the Reformation. Most historians have explained the sharpness of this divergence by saying that it was caused by the rise of rationalism and the scientific outlook toward the end of the seventeenth century. This judgment is still generally valid, but it does not account for the fact that in history there is as much continuity as discontinuity,

* Reprinted with the permission of the author and the editors of *Church History* (XXIX, 1960, 424–437, with omissions).

as much continuation as change. This truth is illustrated by Professor Mosse, who shows in the following essay how certain streams of radical Christian thought, particularly in England during the civil war period (1642–49), flowed from the seventeenth century into the eighteenth and in so doing prepared the way for the relatively widespread acceptance of the peculiarly eighteenth-century religious belief known as Deism.

The relationship between Christianity and the Enlightenment presents a subtle and difficult problem. No historian has as yet fully answered the important question of how the world view of the eighteenth century is related to that of traditional Christianity. It is certain, however, that the deism of that century rejected traditional Christianity as superstitious and denied Christianity a monopoly upon religious truth. The many formal parallels which can be drawn between Enlightenment and Christianity cannot obscure this fact. From the point of view of historical Christianity, both Protestant and Catholic, the faith of the Enlightenment was blasphemy. It did away with a personal God, it admitted no supernatural above the natural, it denied the relevance of Christ's redemptive task in this world. This essay attempts to discover whether traditional Christian thought itself did not make a contribution to the Enlightenment.

It has always been realized that Christian antecedents to the Enlightenment existed, but these have been sought exclusively in the development of rational theology. Both Tulloch and Cassirer have dealt with the Christian origins of the Enlightenment in these terms, while Cantimori has stated that the movement took its start from Socinianism.[1] The purpose of this essay is to suggest quite another kind of Christian thought which went into the making of the Enlightenment. Protestant radicalism seems to entail a development of thought which could lead to deistic conclusions, and, in the two cases we have singled out as examples, certainly did so. Puritan England offers the best field of investigation because here Protestant radicalism expressed itself with a freedom which was denied elsewhere. It also enables us to compare the ideas of Puritan radicals with another stream of thought which went into the making of the Enlightenment, that of seventeenth-century deism.

The parallels between the Enlightenment and this deistic stream of thought, which had long lost touch with Christian beliefs, are close and obvious. These seventeenth century deists also denied the existence of a personal God and substituted for him the primacy of nature. They

[1] See bibliographical note at end of this selection.

rejected Christ and believed that man's soul was wholly mortal. Contemporaries called them "atheists," but in reality they were deists, for God did play a role in their thought. These men were continuing and deepening ideas inherited from classical and Renaissance times. The centers of that movement were in Italy and France. It is necessary to compare this movement with that deism which we find in Puritan England, for it is certainly possible that ideas which caused so much controversy on the Continent should penetrate across the channel and influence Puritan Deists.

We will attempt to show, however, that these continental ideas came to England in a very limited form and that the deism of our Puritan examples cannot be explained through such influences. Nevertheless, we shall also attempt to show that the Puritans we have singled out paralleled in their thought that of the famous Italian and French Deists. It will be our conclusion that they reached such a position from within their own framework of Puritan thought and that, therefore, such deism could originate in a Christian tradition far removed from rational theology. In order to prove our contention it is necessary first to clarify the deistic stream of thought on the Continent which provided such an obvious ingredient for the deists of the Enlightenment.

These ideas were based, in large part, upon a heterodox interpretation of Aristotle, concepts derived from Averroism, and an important revival of Stoic thought. The consequences which could be drawn from such a mixture of ideas can best be illustrated through Lucillo Vanini (1585–1619), whom the century branded as the "Eagle of Atheists." His fundamental concept, indeed that of all these deists, was the Averroistian idea of the "removed God" who is represented on earth by nature. God does not interfere with nature; it is ruled by certain unchangeable and fixed laws. Man removed from God is, in the Stoic sense, thrown back upon his own moral and ethical self-sufficiency. Vanini came to the conclusion that it was not God but nature which had created man. What then of man's soul? Vanini tended to deny its immortality, though he hesitated upon this point on which other deists were not to hesitate. For example, Caesarius Cremonini (1550–1631) in his lectures at Padua followed the same line of thought as Vanini, but added that man's soul was mortal. This famous teacher could build on the tradition of his university, which had labored to release Aristotle from that Christianity which had enveloped him during the middle ages. Cremonini based himself upon Aristotle's idea that the internal and external faculties of man must be considered jointly.

Christ had no place in such doctrine. For these men, both Christ and Moses were impostors who had tricked mankind. Vanini saw in Christ an exemplification of Machiavelli's dictum that the unarmed prophet must necessarily fail. In France, Théophile de Viau (1590–1626) was to build some of his poems around the theme of Christ the imposter, as did the tract *De Tribus Imposteribus,* written during the century. Machiavelli also provided the source for Moses as an "Archpolitic," a view many a writer had been at pains to refute. When Louis Machon, Canon of Toul, made a favorable comparison of Machiavelli and Scripture for Cardinal Richelieu (1640), Moses emerged as the prime example that a prophet of God can also be a Machiavellian. These men rejected all revealed religion. Vanini believed that such faith was a hypocritical invention to keep the common people in check. As for religion, Théophile wrote to his Huguenot brother, it was time that man threw off ideas born out of the fears of a child.

To these concepts of the deists we must add another facet of their thought which has been given the name "libertinage." This word had meant, in the sixteenth century, those who were filled with the "holy spirit" and thus thought themselves free from any ecclesiastical discipline. Now it came to be applied to those deists who seemed to justify moral laxness. This is of special importance, for it was the libertine element of deism which was to penetrate Puritan England from continental sources. Théophile de Viau provided the classical example of deism leading to libertinage. If nature was the destiny which created and dominated man, then man must not oppose himself to nature. From this idea it was only a step to the Epicurean concept that the passions of the body force the movements of the soul. Théophile took that step and in consequence came to believe that man must not force his passions but must live according to his own nature. The result was a justification for the flouting of accepted conventions; the moral laxness of Théophile and his band of disciples caused much scandal at the court of Louis XIII.

Théophile's ideas were popularized by the *Quatraine Du Déiste* (1622). This poem restated the libertine ingredient in deism by using a simple line of argument which started from God's perfection. Since He was perfection and goodness, God would not inflict misery on man, nor would He be bothered with those miseries which men made for themselves. Because of this, man should enjoy himself on earth while awaiting paradise. God was removed from the tribulations of the world, nature governed on earth, and man had to follow his own nature at all times.

Heresy travels, and elements of deism had traveled to England long before the opening of the seventeenth century. Did it accelerate its pace in the age of Théophile and Vanini when so many continental writers were becoming deeply concerned with this un-Christian movement? It is now that we must note in what manner the ideas represented by these men may have penetrated across the channel.

While on the Continent a growing body of literature was concerned with Vanini and Théophile, in England deism as connected with the "Eagle of Atheists" or the "Prince of Libertines" was of little interest. Yet both had visited England. Archbishop Abbott befriended Vanini as a Carmelite monk who had seen the Anglican light, but not for long, for Vanini seems to have preached his deistic doctrine in London's Italian church. This resulted in his leaving England for the more congenial atmosphere of the Languedoc, where many of the nobility shared his beliefs. Théophile also came to England as part of an embassy sent by Louis XIII. James I refused to receive him, but the Duke of Buckingham did. From that time on, there sprang up an interesting relationship between the Duke and the libertine French poet. When Théophile was briefly imprisoned for his scandalous views and behavior, the Duke of Buckingham interceded with Louis XIII on his behalf. The poet, in turn, thanked the Duke for so openly taking his side in Paris. Already during his visit to England Théophile had presented the Duke with some verses.

In this connection it is important to point out that Théophile's deism, with its libertinage, found initial support in the sophisticated society at the royal court. The poet always managed to secure powerful patronage. In Paris this role was taken first by the Duke of Luynes and then by the Duke of Montmorency; in England apparently the Duke of Buckingham fulfilled that function in spite of the pious airs he was accustomed to assume when it suited his purpose. This continental deism flourished in court society and at universities like Padua. Those involved were either of high birth or men of learning. They thought of themselves as an aristocracy and boasted that the simple folk could never appreciate their teaching. We will show later how this contrasted with those English deists who came from a Christian tradition which had quite different roots from the thought of Théophile or Vanini.

The visits of these men to England seemed to have had little effect in spreading their influence. What about their works themselves? Vanini's were not translated, though excerpts existed in manuscript form. John Donne owned a copy of his works, and John Burton mentioned him in passing. Théophile's poems did not find a translator either, though he did visit England once more, not in person but through Charles Sorel's novel *Francion* (tr. 1655). In considering this novel it will become clear that it was the libertine element of this deism that had appeal in England, rather than the other important facets of this body of thought. *Francion* was a "comical history" which centered around the life of Théophile. Sorel revised the work several times in order to inject a moralizing tone into this book which praised libertinage. The English version contained these revisions. Yet the libertinism which remains was strong enough, as the adventures of Francion flouted all accepted morality.

If Vanini's works were not translated, other Italian deists were represented in Puritan England. While at least two of Cremonini's lectures circulated in manuscript, it was again not the deistic philosophy but deistic libertinism which was presented in translations. The works which are relevant here are those produced by the Venetian *Academia della Incogniti*. The members of this Academy were the young aristocrats of the city who turned to the writing of literature under the influence of the ideas of Vanini and Cremonini. Many of their works did represent a specifically deistic philosophy, but this was not the way in which they reached English readers. Their works suffered the same fate that had overtaken the Italian novellae in Painter's and Fenton's collections of the previous century. They were injected with a morality not to be found in the original work. Yet the libertine trend of the Academy was present in the *Choice Novels and Amorous Tales written by the most refined Witts in Italy* (tr. 1652), the collected novellae of the Academy.

Ferrante Palavicino's contributions to this work were openly libertine in that they glorified moral laxness. As in *Francion,* this laxness shaded over into blasphemy. Palavicino applied religious imagery to the lusts of the flesh in order to ridicule the divine. To seventeenth century Europe Palavicino represented Vanini's successor as the "Eagle of Atheists" long before he became transformed into a champion of free thought by Stendhal in his *Charterhouse of Parma.* This Italian example demonstrates once more that it was this libertine trend of deistic thought which had special appeal.

It is possible to suggest two reasons why this should be so. First, in Puritan England these novellae and romances were undoubtedly good reading. They must have provided a welcome change from literature of devotion or of moral exhortation. Second, libertinism was directed against hypocrisy in religion. Thus Francion praised the libertines with their "free and galant humour," even though they were apt to be inconstant in judgment. Sorel extended his attacks upon hypocrisy from religion to politics and the court. Francion wanted to associate with those who "laugh and love." In such companions there was more contentment than could be found in churches or in politics. Palavicino also made fun of the hypocrisy of religion. All this was, of course, strongly implied in the doctrine of the impostors and in the concept of religion as a utilitarian device. Deism then did not penetrate across the channel by attacking Christ or by rejecting religion in favor of natural-ism and the mortality of the soul. Libertinism, growing out of this thought, was directed against hypocrisy, and in this, Puritan England may have found a very congenial parallelism to its own concern with "fundamentals."

The ideology of continental deism has now been clarified through the example of its leading exponents. We have seen how these ideas came to England in a very limited and partial manner through libertin-ism. Yet in Puritan England there existed deistic thought corresponding to that of the Continent. The origin of this thought must not be sought in the continental examples, but in the beliefs of Christianity itself. Christianity in this case is not defined as that rational theology which undoubtedly existed in Revolutionary England and which in its turn influenced English deism, but rather as the Christian thought of radical Puritanism. Thomas Edwards in his comprehensive catalogue of heresies (1645) included as a current heresy the belief that the soul was mortal and that faith could not transcend nature. Moreover, he quoted Philip Nye to the effect that the "denying of Christ was a growing opinion." How did Christian beliefs lead to such conclusions?

Throughout his *Gangraena* Thomas Edwards concentrated his ire upon one of the Puritan ministers, Thomas Webbe. Webbe was a mem-ber of a radical Puritan sect known as the Ranters. This was a loosely defined body of men who denied the validity of the Church, scrip-tures, worship and dogma. They had evolved from that religious group which contemporaries called the "Seekers," people who believed that there was no visible apostolic power among men in the present state of apostasy. They sought for God to give them a visible demonstration of hope through the sending of an angel or apostle to earth. As early as 1617 John Morton had applied the epithet "libertine" to the Seekers and charged them with speaking against Christ in maintaining that none are saved by the blood of Christ, which was of no particular value. This Seeker thought was given an ecstatic and mystical twist by the Ranters, who felt that the time for true revival of prophecy was at hand.

Ranters believed that "every creature in the first state of creation was God, and every creature is God. . . ." Man was an emanation of God, but man's return to God had to await the coming of the resurrection. Between the "first creation" and that expected event, man and the world were cut off from direct divine intervention. Only to His prophets like Muggleton and John Reeve did God speak directly in order that they might prepare the world for His distinct appearance in the clouds of heaven. These Ranters talked about the existence of two worlds. The earth is the lower world, so polluted by sin that its processes of life are removed from God's concern. This meant that man's soul as well as his body were conceived by an instinct of nature and not by an infusion of God's spirit. The soul was as mortal as man's body, a division which makes possible a materialist concept of the world below—until the resurrection.

Christ, however, seemed important in Ranter doctrine as far as the revival of true prophecy was concerned. When Muggleton and Reeves wrote their *Divine Looking-Glass* (1656) they thought themselves inspired by the "fiery glorious spirit of Jesus Christ." At one point in his development Webbe gave an accurate formulation of this Christianity when he preached that Christ and his spirit were infused into the souls of those who had faith. The growing Ranter opposition to Christ, which went back to their Seeker origin, was reinforced by two developments. First was the attack upon these radicals by the orthodox. The attempts of the Presbyterians to impose their theology upon Puritan England led to a denial, in some cases, not only of the Presbyterian ideas on predestination, but also of their concept of Christ.

Secondly, the Ranters were attacked for their denial of the traditionally practiced worship of Christ. In consequence they began in turn to sharpen their attack upon such worship, and especially upon the essence of this worship, the Eucharist. Thus in one Ranter meeting, "one of them took a piece of beef in his hand, tearing it asunder said to another, 'this is the flesh of Christ, take and eat.'" Such mockery of the Eucharist was, as we have seen, duplicated in the libertine literature which did come to England. From ridiculing Christian worship, it was only a step to an attack on Christ himself. Moverover, the primacy of God in Ranter thought made it easy to obscure the function of Christ. Muggleton and Reeve rejected the Trinity, fusing Christ and God into one identity. Christ was God, clothed for a brief time with "flesh and bone." Thus Christ could have no separate and delegated redemptive power in this world. By 1652 it was charged against Webbe that while he had called Christ the greatest ordinance set up by God, he had also asserted that "saints" could live unto God without those ordinances. George Fox, who knew the Ranters well, accused them of having jumped a step in their religious development. They started out as God's "and never came through the prophets, nor Moses' house, nor Christ who is the end of all oathes." Thus Webbe eventually came to call Christ an impostor, since an almighty and powerful God would never have trusted a weak and crucified Christ. He, a Puritan minister, arrived at the same doctrine of the impostor as that held by the continental deists, but he started from a Christian context.

Mooveover, the concentration on God combined with the removal of God from the active affairs of the world, on which we have touched above, gave man an ethical self-sufficiency reminiscent of Théophile. Many Ranters believed that as all power comes from God, and He is goodness, therefore human sin "has its conception only in the imagination." Lawrence Clarkson summed this up well. Since all power was from God, all man's acts were produced by that power. Because God's power produced man's actions and God was goodness as well as perfection, man's acts must necessarily be good. "There is no act whatsoever that is impure in God or sinful before God." Such ideas led to a libertine and deistic position. God was removed from man's daily actions in any ethical or moral sense because He had no immediate interest in them. Webbe repeated Clarkson's point and added that God could not be displeased or angry with man. If God were pleased at one moment and angry at the next, He would be changeable and not perfect. This very view of God as the source of all goodness and perfection tended to divorce him from man, and the human abandoned to his own devices could be viewed as wholly mortal. As Webbe put it, all things shall have an end and only God will remain forever.

Webbe reached a position parallel to that of Vanini or Théophile on the mortality of the soul, the denial of Christ, and the "removed" God of deism. He added the libertine element of that thought which in any case was explicit in the Ranter position. Webbe flaunted his adulteries even under persecution and was denounced as a lover of "music and mixed dancing." What is missing in Webbe as compared with the continentals was the emphasis upon nature. The very God-centeredness of the Ranter doctrine, which facilitated Webbe's deism, prevented him from injecting nature between God and man, as man's real and dominating destiny.

Webbe, then, came to his conclusion from what was an undogmatic and mystical Christianity. Richard Overton reached his conclusions through a similar Christian tradition; however, Overton emphasized in his thought one component of Puritan radicalism which Webbe lacked. He had a chiliastic view of the world and it is this that enabled him, despite his deism, to retain a Christian framework of thought. Moreover, Overton was also, unlike Webbe, influenced by a Christian nature mysticism which enabled him to stress nature as the continental deists stressed it. Yet despite all these differences, both Overton and Webbe demonstrate how a deistic mode of thought could arise from within a Christian tradition and not from overtly anti-Christian or rational Christian thought. Both shared the background of a Puritan radicalism as typified by the Seekers and above all by the Ranters. However, the special interest in Overton lies in the fusion he made between Christianity and deism. In his ideology an essentially hostile mode of thought existed side by side with an emphasized Christianity. He would not have understood the dichtomy between Christianity and the Enlightenment, though he shows how a professed Christian ideology could evolve into deism. Thomas Webbe had stripped the Christian element from his thought at the end; Overton shows that at one point in the evolution of radical Christian thought it could coexist with deism, and indeed through such coexistence provides additional proof of the Christian component of that movement.

Overton's thought was closely linked to that of the Soul Sleepers, who believed that body and soul died together and were resurrected together at the last judgment. This belief in the mortality of the soul was similar to that of Théophile and Vanini except that this mortality was temporary, i.e., it lasted only up to the resurrection. Though many have thought that the Soul Sleepers originated with Overton's *Man's Mortality,* this belief actually had a long history behind it before Overton wrote his book in 1644. Calvin's first theological tract of 1534 had been directed against such beliefs. Doumergue believed that these Soul Sleepers had thousands of adherents in France during Calvin's lifetime. Barclay held that Ranter origins went beyond the Seekers to one of Calvin's principal opponents, Antoine Pocque, who was also a Soul Sleeper. If this be true, there existed a definite link between the doctrines of the Ranters and those of the Soul Sleepers. There can be no doubt that this belief had a continuous history from Calvin to Overton, though little is known about it.

The ideas of the Soul Sleepers were closely associated not only with the Ranters, but also with both the Baptists and the Mennonites. The Baptists in Italy and France had at times adopted Soul Sleeping; such an association also existed in England, for we hear that in Kent and Sussex Baptists were linked to a sect known as the Soul Sleepers. Overton, who because a Baptist when he came to England, never left this church, whose institutions he thought were "holy and good." In his youth he had joined the Mennonite Dutch Waterland Church. His application for membership in that church already showed that stress upon the resurrection which was to be important in his later thought, though it was still combined with an equal emphasis upon the Trinity and upon grief for sin which will be forgiven by Christ. This stress upon the resurrection was also a part of the religious thought of John Smythe, the leader of the English faction in that particular Mennonite Church. Smythe combined the resurrection with the idea that men in their graves rest from their work as God did from his. Though Smythe believed the soul to be immortal, the concept of the God who rests from his work was important in the deistic thought of Overton. Smythe based himself on Hebrews 4:10, which states that he who has entered into rest, rests from his own work as God did from his. Smythe's interpretation may seem straightforward, but Calvin had taken quite another note of this passage. For him, God could never rest from his labors, and he interpreted the word "rest" as an exhortation to man to cast off his appetites, renounce himself, and follow God. Smythe did not remove God from the concerns of the world, but another member of the congregation, John Canne, did combine such ideas with Seeker and Ranter thought which had a foothold in English Mennonite churches. John Canne was the printer of *Man's Mortality*. He believed that God did rest removed from His world because for the last years there had been no true witnesses in His church. Now the time for resurrection was at hand. Holding these beliefs, he became a Fifth Monarchy man. There is little doubt that here Overton was exposed to an intellectual atmosphere which had direct influence upon *Man's Mortality*. The resurrection at the last judgment was the beginning of the immortality of the soul. Prior to that day, man's mortal soul was governed by nature, which ran as well without God's interference as it would with His help.

Ranter doctrines of nature were also influenced by the Christian nature mysticism of Jacob Boehme. For this German cobbler, Scripture could only be understood through such lessons as nature could teach man. Man's anticipation of the second coming could be expressed in his efforts to fuse with God and Christ through such lessons as nature could teach man. This was a pantheistic ideal, which put nature into the center of a Christian and mystical experience. Boehme's view of nature involved a dualism that was similar to Overton's thought. Nature was both good and bad, but the goodness of nature could only be seen by that man who had been reborn through the fusing of his spirit with God through Christ. Since for Overton nature was corrupt, there could be no perfection as long as nature, and man as part of nature, were divorced from the divine. These pantheistic ideas could be modified through a stress upon the chiliastic end. Once the importance of nature had been stated in this way, it was simple for both Overton and the Ranters to take God out of the immediate realm of the world which was then governed by nature. God was relegated to a distant waiting position until the time was ripe for him to return to the world in the final days of judgment. The only power governing man's soul until that day was the power of nature. This, however, did not mean that God was powerless.

Overton's ideology was dominated by his chiliasm, a fact which has been overlooked by later historians who have been unduly astonished by his deism. Man was generated, propagated, and ruled by nature, but this would be changed in the end when God through Christ would make immortality possible. Despite his correspondence to the continentals, Overton omitted the attacks upon Christ just as Webbe omitted the ingredients of deistic naturalism. To be sure Overton believed that in the affairs of this world neither God nor Christ played a part, but both were essential for the chiliastic end. Overton believed in Christ. Christ had existed, was resurrected, and went to heaven, which he identified with the sun. In contrast, Vanini believed Christ had, after his failure, gone to die in the desert. Overton's chiliasm allowed him to surround his naturalism and deism with the Christian concept of the final goal of life. His deism was not dependent upon continental models; it sprang from certain tendencies in radical Christian thought.

The comparison between the deism which came from a Christian tradition unrelated to rational theology and that deism which was such an important movement in France and Italy has brought out the similarity between them. Théophile and Vanini on the one hand, Webbe and Overton on the other, came to identical conclusions about the mortality of the soul and the noninterference of God in the affairs of this world. Webbe agreed in the rejection of Christ as an impostor, and Overton, who retained Christ, shared the deistic view of nature. These two streams of thought seem to flow parallel to each other for, as we saw, the ideas of the continentals came to England stripped of their explicit philosophical base.

If the undogmatic, mystical, and chiliastic Christianity of these Puritan Radicals could lead to such deist thought, then they also contributed to a more general change in the direction of seventeenth century Christianity. For at the same time casuistic Divinity was introducing a more realistic orientation from within Christian orthodoxy.

The Presbyterian Westminister Assembly, so hostile to the sects, was exhorted by one of their numbers to vote a convenient proposition first and then find the matching Scriptural text for it. Louis Machon was not alone in seeing no contradiction between the ways of Machiavelli and those of God. Moreover, Calvinist orthodoxy was pointing towards a rationalism which, in the next century, would lead one minister to say that if God could not defend His happiness against evil men except by using a lie, then He would do so. It is this more general loosening of the traditional Christian thought and ethic which gives significance to the fact that such a development could also take place within radical Christianity, close to popular piety. Here too the Christian framework of thought could be used, and was used, to defeat its own professed objectives. In this manner Puritan radicalism could provide one of the stimuli that went into the making of the Enlightenment.

BIBLIOGRAPHY

Delio Cantimori, *Italienische Haeretiker der Spätenrenaissance* (Basel: 1949). Ernst Cassirer, *The Philosophy of the Enlightenment* (Princeton, N.J.: 1951). John Tulloch, *Rational Theology and Christian Philosophy in England in the Seventeenth Century* (2 vols.; Edinburgh: 1872). See also Basil Willey, *The Seventeenth Century Background* (London: 1934). [The Editor.]

THE TOUCH OF COLD PHILOSOPHY *

Basil Willey†

If, as we saw in the preceding selection, continuity played a part in preparing the way for eighteenth-century changes in religious outlook, one of the important developments in the long history of the West was the great explosion of scientific achievement that occurred throughout the seventeenth century and reached its climax in Sir Isaac

---

* Reprinted with the permission of the publishers, Stanford University Press. Copyright 1951 by the Board of Trustees of the Leland Stanford Junior University.

† Basil Willey, "The Touch of Cold Philosophy," *The Seventeenth Century: Studies in the History of English Thought and Literature from Bacon to Pope,* Richard Foster Jones and Others Writing in His Honor (Stanford, Calif.: 1951), pp. 369–376, with omissions. [Editor's note.]

Newton's scientific writings. The impact of these intellectual discoveries had an effect that, in some instances at least, altered men's beliefs almost overnight. If the speed of change has sometimes been over-emphasized, still we cannot deny that change existed and that it had a relatively sudden as well as significant effect. The way in which this change manifested itself in eighteenth-century thought is the subject of Professor Willey's essay.

In order to get a bird's-eye view of any century it is quite useful to imagine it as a stretch of country, or a landscape, which we are looking at from a great height, let us say from an aeroplane. If we view the seventeenth century in this way we shall be struck immediately by the great contrast between the scenery and even the climate of its earlier and that of its later years. At first we get mountain-ranges, torrents, and all the picturesque interplay of alternating storm and brightness; then, farther on, the land slopes down to a richly cultivated plain, broken for a while by outlying heights and spurs, but finally becoming level country, watered by broad rivers, adorned with parks and mansions, and lit up by steady sunshine. The mountains connect backwards with the central mediaeval Alps, and the plain leads forwards with little break into our own times. To drop the metaphor before it begins to be misleading, we may say that the seventeenth century was an age of transition, and although every century can be so described, the seventeenth deserves this label better than most, because it lies between the Middle Ages and the modern world. It witnessed one of the greatest changes which have ever taken place in men's ways of thinking about the world they live in.

Merely to glance at this historical landscape is enough to make one seek some explanation of these changes. If the developments had conflicted with each other we might have put them down to a number of different causes, but since they all seem to be setting in one direction it is natural to suppose that they were all due to one common underlying cause. There are various ways of accounting for historical changes: some people believe, for instance, that economic causes are at the bottom of everything, and that the way men earn their living, and the way in which wealth is produced and distributed, determine how men think and write and worship. Others believe that ideas, rather than material conditions, are what control history, and that the important question to ask about any period is what men then believed to be true, what their philosophy and religion were like. There is something to be said on both sides, but we are concerned with a simpler question. We know that the greatest intellectual change in modern history was completed during the seventeenth century: was that change of such a kind as to explain all those parallel movements we have mentioned? Would it have helped that drift towards prose and reason, towards classicism, enlightenment, and toleration? The great intellectual change was that known as the Scientific Revolution, and I think the answer to these questions is, Yes. It is not my present purpose to describe that Revolution, or to discuss any of the great discoveries which produced it. My intention is only to consider some of the effects it had upon men's thoughts, imaginations, and feelings, and consequently upon their ways of expressing themselves. The discoveries—I am thinking mainly of the Copernican astronomy and the laws of motion as explored by Galileo and fully formulated by Newton—shocked men into realizing that things were not as they had always seemed, and that the world they were living in was really quite different from what they had been taught to suppose. When the crystal spheres of the old world-picture were shattered, and the earth was shown to be one of many planets rolling through space, it was not everyone who greeted this revelation with enthusiasm as Giordano Bruno did. Many felt lost and confused, because the old picture had not only seemed obviously true to common sense, but was confirmed by Scripture and by Aristotle, and hallowed by the age-long approval of the Church. What Matthew Arnold said about the situation in the nineteenth century applies also to the seventeenth: religion had attached its emotion to certain supposed facts, and now the facts were failing it. This note of loss can be heard in Donne's well-known lines:

> And new philosophy calls all in doubt;
> The element of fire is quite put out;
> The sun is lost, and th'earth, and no man's wit
> Can well direct him where to look for it.

Not only "the element of fire," but the very distinction between heaven and earth had vanished—the distinction, I mean, between the perfect and incorruptible celestial bodies from the moon upwards, and the imperfect and corruptible terrestrial bodies below it. New stars had appeared, which showed that the heavens could change, and the telescope revealed irregularities in the moon's surface—that is, the moon was not a perfect sphere, as a celestial body should be. So Sir Thomas Browne could write:

> While we look for incorruption in the heavens, we find they are but like the earth;—durable in their main bodies, alterable in their parts;

whereof, besides comets and new stars, perspectives begin to tell tales, and the spots that wander about the sun, with Phaeton's favour, would make clear conviction.

Naturally it took a long time for these new ideas to sink in, and Milton still treats the old and the new astronomies as equally acceptable alternatives. The Copernican scheme, however, was generally accepted by the second half of the century. By that time the laws governing the motion of bodies on earth had also been discovered, and finally it was revealed by Newton that the law whereby an apple falls to the ground is the very same as that which keeps the planets in their courses. The realization of this vast unifying idea meant a complete re-focussing of men's ideas about God, Nature, and Man, and the relationships between them. The whole cosmic movement, in the heavens and on earth, must now be ascribed, no longer to a divine pressure acting through the *primum mobile,* and to angelic intelligences controlling the spheres, but to a gravitational pull which could be mathematically calculated. The universe turned out to be a Great Machine, made up of material parts which all moved through space and time according to the strictest rules of mechanical causation. That is to say, since every effect in nature had a physical cause, no room or need was left for supernatural agencies, whether divine or diabolical; every phenomenon was explicable in terms of matter and motion, and could be mathematically accounted for or predicted.

I referred just now to some of the immediate effects of the "New Philosophy"; let me conclude by hinting at a few of its ultimate effects. First, it produced a distrust of all tradition, a determination to accept nothing as true merely on authority, but only after experiment and verification. You find Bacon rejecting the philosophy of the mediaeval Schoolmen, Browne writing a long exposure of popular errors and superstitions (such as the belief that a toad had a jewel in its head, or that an elephant had no joints in its legs), Descartes resolving to doubt everything—even his own senses—until he can come upon something clear and certain, which he finally finds in the fact of his own existence as a thinking being. Thus, the chief intellectual task of the seventeenth century became the winnowing of truth from error, fact from fiction or fable. Gradually a sense of confidence, and even exhilaration, set in; the universe seemed no longer mysterious or frightening; everything in it was explicable and comprehensible. Comets and eclipses were no longer dreaded as portents of disaster; witchcraft was dismissed as an old wives' tale. This new feeling of security is expressed in Pope's epitaph on Newton:

Nature and Nature's laws lay hid in night;
God said, *Let Newton be!* and all was light!

How did all this affect men's religious beliefs? The effect was very
different from that of Darwinism on nineteenth-century religion. In
the seventeenth century it was felt that science had produced a
conclusive demonstation of God, by showing the evidence of His
wisdom and power in the Creation. True, God came to be thought of
rather as an abstract First Cause than as the personal, ever-present
God of religion; the Great Machine implied the Great Mechanic,
but after making the machine and setting it in motion God had, as it
were, retired from active superintendence, and left it to run by its
own laws without interference. But at a time when inherited religious
sentiment was still very powerful, the idea that you could look up
through Nature to Nature's God seemed to offer an esecape from
one of the worst legacies of the past—religious controversy and sectarian
intolerance. Religion had been endangered by inner conflicts; what
could one believe, when the Churches were all at daggers drawn?
Besides, the secular and rational temper brought in by the new science
soon began to undermine the traditional foundations of belief. If
nothing had ever happened which could not be explained by natural,
physical causes, what of the supernatural and miraculous events recorded in the Bible? This was a disturbing thought, and even in the
seventeenth century there were a few who began to doubt the literal
truth of some of the Biblical narratives. But it was reserved for the
eighteenth century to make an open attack upon the miraculous
elements in Christianity, and to compare the Old Testament Jehovah
disparagingly with the "Supreme Being" or "First Cause" of philosophy.
For the time it was possible to feel that science was pious, because it
was simply engaged in studying God's own handiwork, and because
whatever is disclosed seemed a further proof of His almighty skill as
designer of the universe. Science also gave direct access to God, whereas
Church and creed involved you in endless uncertainties and difficulties.

However, some problems and doubts arose to disturb the prevailing
optimism. If the universe was a material mechanism, how could Man
be fitted into it—Man, who had always been supposed to have a free
will and an immortal soul? Could it be that these were illusions after
all? Not many faced up to this, though Hobbes did say that the soul
was only a function of the body, and denied the freedom of the will.
What was more immediately serious, especially for poetry and religion,
was the new tendency to discount all the products of the imagination,

and all spiritual insight, as false or fictitious. Everything that was real could be described by mathematical physics as matter in motion, and whatever could not be so described was either unreal or else had not yet been truly explained. Poets and priests had deceived us long enough with vain imaginings; it was now time for the scientists and philosophers to take over, and speak to us, as Sprat says the Royal Society required its members to do, in a "naked, natural" style, bringing all things as close as possible to the "mathematical plainness." Poets might rave, and priests might try to mystify us, but sensible men would ignore them, preferring good sense, and sober, prosaic demonstration. It was said at the time that philosophy (which then included what we call science) had cut the throat of poetry. This does not mean that no more good poetry could then be produced: after all, Dryden and Pope were both excellent poets. But, when all has been said, they do lack visionary power: their merits are those of their age—sense, wit, brilliance, incisiveness, and point. It is worth noticing that when the Romantic Movement began a hundred years later, several of the leading poets attacked science for having killed the universe and turned man into a reasoning machine. But no such thoughts worried the men of the Augustan age; their prevailing feeling was satisfaction at living in a world that was rational through and through, a world that had been explained favourably, explained piously, and explained by an Englishman. The modern belief in progress takes its rise at this time; formerly it had been thought that perfection lay in antiquity, and that subsequent history was one long decline. But now that Bacon, Boyle, Newton, and Locke had arisen, who could deny that the ancients had been far surpassed? Man could now hope to control his environment as never before, and who could say what triumphs might not lie ahead? Even if we feel that the victory of science was then won at the expense of some of man's finer faculties, we can freely admit that it brought with it many good gifts as well—tolerance, reasonableness, release from fear and superstition—and we can pardon, and even envy, that age for its temporary self-satisfaction.

BIBLIOGRAPHY

Edwin A. Burtt, *The Metaphysical Foundations of Modern Physical Science* (2nd rev. ed.; London: 1932). Francis Oakley, "Christian Theology and the Newtonian Science: the Rise of the Concept of the Laws of Nature," *Church History*, XXX (1961), 433–457. Richard S. Westfall, *Science and Religion in Seventeenth-Century England* (New Haven:

1958). Basil Willey, *The Eighteenth Century Background* (London: 1940). For this and succeeding sections see also Franklin L. Baumer, *Religion and the Rise of Scepticism* (New York: 1960). [The Editor.]

THE UNITY OF THE FRENCH ENLIGHTENMENT *

Peter Gay

The "age of the Enlightenment" is a term that has been used for some time to describe the outlook and attitudes of a large part of the eighteenth century. The term implies a value judgment in the sense that many individuals, and particularly that group of the French intellectual elite known as the philosophes, *looked upon their own time as more "enlightened" and "progressive" than preceding periods of history. In general, the age is usually characterized as anti-Christian and intellectually rebellious. In the following essay Professor Gay stresses further our theme of continuity in spite of change by calling attention to the fact that the* philosophes, *despite their militant impiety, were a part of the time in which they lived. Even as they criticized existing religious ideas and practices they were still influenced by a common outlook and a historical tradition shared by Christians and sceptics alike.*

The *philosophes* . . . much as they wished to change it, were at home in their world. To divide the [eighteenth] century into two sharply defined forces—subversive *philosophes* against the orthodox—may be convenient and dramatic, but it is also much too simple. There were moments of crisis when two parties crystallized and Catholics squared off against unbelievers, but subtler and more pervasive than hostility were the ties that bound the *philosophes* to their society. They edited respectable magazines, flattered royal mistresses, wrote unexceptionable entertainments, and held responsible posts.

Nor was their attachment to the existing order based solely on

* Reprinted with the permission of the author from *History* (No. 3, September, 1960, 7–28, with omissions).

calculation: they shared with literate Christians a religious education, a love for the classics of Roman and French literature, and an affection for the pleasures of cultivated leisure. Seeking to distinguish themselves, they did not wish to abolish all distinctions. When they participated in politics, they often supported one orthodox party against another: Montesquieu the *parlements* against the king, Voltaire the king against the *parlements*. While they helped to prepare the way for the Jacobins, they were not Jacobins themselves.

Their attachment was strengthened by their association with a spectrum of would-be *philosophes,* half-*philosophes,* or Christians liberal enough to tolerate, or even to enjoy, men whose doctrines they rejected. Hangers-on who basked in borrowed glory or second-hand notoriety smuggled *philosophes'* letters, arranged for theatrical claques, and offered true friendship in a quarrelsome world. Strategically placed officials stood between *philosophes* and the severities of the law, and good Christians who dabbled in higher criticism or polite anticlericalism spread philosophic doctrine in respectable circles. In a word, the *philosophes* were deeply embedded in the texture of their society.

Yet this did not prevent them from being at war with it at the same time. The *philosophes* never developed a coherent political program or even a consistent line of political tactics, but their polemics called for a France profoundly different from the country in which they lived—France after, not before, 1791. The regime could make concessions: boredom, a lost sense of purpose, could make many a bourgeois, priest, or aristocrat receptive to subversive propaganda. But aggressive deism or materialism, doctrines of the rule of law, complete toleration, and subordination of church to state—these tenets could not be assimilated by the old order. To neglect either side of their dual situation is to make the *philosophes* more revolutionary or more conservative than in fact they were.

This tension which is yet not alienation places not only the *philosophes* in their century, it places the century itself. To say that the eighteenth century was an age of contradictions, is to say nothing: all ages have this characteristic in common. We must be specific: eighteenth-century France was a Christian culture that was rapidly losing its Christian vocation without being fully aware of it.

"One day," writes Paul Hazard, "the French people, almost to a man, were thinking like Bossuet. The day after, they were thinking like Voltaire." This is doubly wrong. The *philosophes* had much opposition among the educated and the powerful. While the writings of Montesquieu and Voltaire and Diderot have survived, those of their adversaries have not, but survival is an unreliable guide to the intellectual map of the past: in the age of Louis XV Christianity had many a persuasive and intelligent defender. Moreover, we cannot properly speak of a "French people" in the eighteenth century. Most Frenchmen were wholly untouched by the Enlightenment and lived, as it were, in an earlier century. They believed in witches, applied spells, used home remedies long condemned by physicians, displayed a trust in authority long discarded by the educated, lived and died happily ignorant of the battles among Cartesians and Newtonians.

Yet for men sensitive or educated enough to be aware of intellectual currents, the eighteenth century was a time of turmoil. A whole complex of ideas and experiences, usually lumped together in the slippery word "secularization," came together in the reign of Louis XV to haunt thinking men. The literature of travel offered the spectacle of happy and civilized non-Christian cultures; the demands of international politics forged secular rather than sectarian alliances; the growth of the European economy stimulated the desire for worldly goods; the great discoveries of science suggested the appalling possibility of a universe without God.

Secularization did not mean the death of religion. Eight Frenchmen out of ten—perhaps nine—were uncontaminated by skepticism. Even the businessman or artisan, who greatly benefited from advances in technology, rarely allowed them to affect his faith. Still, what Troeltsch has called the "Church-directed civilization" was crumbling. Christians lived by the image of hierarchy: as God, his angels, and his creatures were arranged in an order of rank, so by analogy the skies, the family, law, society, the Church, were naturally hierarchical.

Now, as natural scientists demonstrated that the hierarchies of terrestrial and celestial motion, or the spheres of the heavens, were absurd, other revolutionaries were exposing the absurdity of other hierarchies.

In this time of trouble the two great hierarchical institutions, the church and the nobility, did little to counteract this exposure. It is easy to exaggerate the worldliness of the eighteenth-century cleric or the uselessness of the eighteenth-century nobleman. Too much has been written about the atheist abbé and the idle marquis. There were many aristocrats who served their country ably, and rose above the interests of their order to advocate truly national policies. Yet as the history of eighteenth-century France demonstrates, the French aristocracy was on the whole unwilling to make the sacrifices necessary to integrate it into a state that demanded some centralization of power and some revision of the tax structure. Born in an age that had given it a social function, the aristocratic caste was losing its vocation, as embittered renegades like the Marquis D'Argenson did not fail to point out.

A similar loss of vocation threatened the Church. Thousands of priests fulfilled their offices with devotion; even some bishops believed in God. But in a time when natural philosophers were offering alternative explanations of the origins of man, the nature of evil, and the purpose of life, the Church needed a firmness of character, adroitness of policy, and above all a unity that it could not muster. Many a young man of talent went into the opposition, and used the dialectical skill and classical learning imparted by his priestly instructors for their destruction.

Still, for all the impiety of the age, religion survived, and one reason for the survival was that the famous war between science and theology did not take place in the simple form familiar to us from the Whig interpretation. The warfare began not between theology and science, but theology and some philosophical consequences drawn from science. It was not necessary to accept D'Alembert's positivism to be a good mathematician; or to be driven by Voltaire's anticlerical spleen to be a good Newtonian. Science, travel, politics, wealth, the great secularizing forces, did their work by indirection, as it were, behind the century's back.

Still they did their work, and they did it in the eighteenth century. In a celebrated book Paul Hazard has expended much learning to establish a crisis in the European conscience before 1715.[1] It is true that practically all the most aggressive ideas of eighteenth-century propagandists had a prehistory, but they did not touch a significant number of people until well after Newton's death in 1727. The typical seventeenth-century scientist was a good Christian: he was a Pascal, not a Hobbes. By separating theology from natural philosophy, or by ingeniously arguing that natural philosophy *supported* theology, seventeenth-century scientists concealed from themselves, as much as from others, the revolutionary implications of their work. It is a commonplace, but one all too often forgotten, that the geniuses from Galileo to Newton lived comfortably with convictions that eighteenth-century *philosophes* would stigmatize as incompatible. John Donne's famous and too much quoted lament that "new philosophy calls all in doubt," was the exceptional response of an exceptional man. In general, the imagination of the century was unaffected, or playfully expanded, by the new universe glimpsed in the new instruments. For Newton,

[1] See bibliography at end of selection. [Editor's note.]

God was active in the universe, occasionally correcting the irregularities of the solar system. The Newtonian heavens proclaimed God's glory.

This happy marriage of theism and science was not dissolved until the eighteenth century, when the discoveries of the age of genius were pushed to their logical conclusion. "Once the foundation of a revolution has been laid down," D'Alembert wrote in the *Encyclopédie*, "it is almost always in the next generation that the revolution is accomplished." Several brilliant French mathematicians, D'Alembert among them, generalized Newton's laws of gravitation far beyond Newton's wishes. By the last quarter of the century, Lagrange and Laplace had established, in elegant equations, the stability of the solar system. The goal of eighteenth-century science had become evident: Newton's physics without Newton's God.

The crisis of secularization, then, was slower and subtler than we have been led to believe. It was also more pervasive. It was not confined to educated Christians, tormented by the startling conclusions of physicists. It was a problem for the *philosophes* themselves. It is not surprising that their anguish has received little attention—they covered it well with urbanity and noisy anticlericalism.

But anguish there was. The *philosophes* had two enemies: the institutions of Christianity and the idea of hierarchy. And they had two problems: God and the masses. Both the enemies and the problems were related and woven into the single task of rethinking their world. The old questions that Christianity had answered so fully for so many men and so many centuries, had to be asked anew: What, as Kant put it, What can I know? What ought I to do? What may I hope?

Science itself did not answer these questions. It only suggested—ever more insistently as the century went on—that the old answers were wrong. Now, the *philosophes* were products of Christian homes and Christian schools. If they became enemies of Christianity, they did so not from indifference or ignorance: they knew their Bible, their catechism, their Church Fathers, their apologetics. And they knew, because it had been drummed into them early, the fate that awaits heretics or atheists in the world to come. Their anticlerical humor therefore has the bitter intimacy of the family joke; to embrace materialism was an act of rejection.

The *philosophes'* crisis was a crisis of freedom. They did not fully understand it, but to the extent that they did understand it, they knew their situation to be filled with terror and delight. They felt the anxiety and exhilaration of the explorer who stands before the unknown. It may not be fair to call to witness Rousseau, whose malaise was perpetual. But the shape of his agony mirrors the agony of his century. Nothing is more pathetic than Rousseau's attempt to rescue at least some comforting aspects of his universe from the icy blasts of Voltaire's cosmic pessimism. "All the subtleties of metaphysics," he wrote Voltaire, seeking to answer the poem on the Lisbon earthquake, "will not make me doubt for a moment the immortality of the soul or a beneficent Providence. I feel it, I believe it, I want it, I hope for it, and I shall defend it to my last breath." But the edifice of Rousseau's faith was flimsily built on illogical hope: the immortality of the soul and a beneficent Providence are articles of faith to which a Christian happily subscribes, but to which the deist, nourished on scientific skepticism, has no right.

Diderot, the most ebullient of *philosophes,* the freest and most inventive of spirits, was driven from position to position and haunted by doubts. Born into a family richly endowed with priests, of pious parents and with a fanatical brother, long toying with entering the priesthood, Diderot moved from Catholicism to theism, from theism to deism, from deism to skepticism, and from skepticism to atheism. But atheism, with its cold determinism, repelled him even though he accepted it as true; while Catholicism, with its colorful ceremony, moved him even though he rejected it as false. Writing to his mistress, Sophie Volland, he cursed the philosophy—his own—that reduced their love to a blind encounter of atoms. "I am furious at being entangled in a confounded philosophy which my mind cannot refrain from approve and my heart from denying."

The materialists of course claimed to be defiantly happy at being cosmic orphans. But the question, If God is dead, what is permitted? was not a question calculated to make men sleep easy.

I am not simply arguing that the *philosophes* were less cheerful than they appeared in their social roles—most of us are. Nor that they suffered personal crises—philosophers, especially young philosophers, often do. I am arguing that the *philosophes'* anguish was related to the crisis in Christian civilization; that (to use different language) whatever childhood experiences made them psychologically vulnerable in adult life, their obsessions, their self-questionings, their anxieties, were poured into their religious, moral, and political speculation.

BIBLIOGRAPHY

F. L. Baumer, *Religion and the Rise of Scepticism.* Carl Becker, *The Heavenly City of the Eighteenth Century Philosophers* (New Haven: 1955). Peter Gay, *Voltaire's Politics: the Poet as Realist* (Princeton: 1959). Paul Hazard,

La crise de la conscience européenne (1680–1715) (Paris: 1935) [Translated as
The European Mind: the Critical Years (New Haven: 1953)]. See also the
same author's La pensée européenne au XVIIIème siècle: de Montesquieu à
Lessing (Paris: 1946) [Translated as European Thought in the Eighteenth
Century from Montesquieu to Lessing (New Haven: 1954)]. Frank E.
Manuel, The Eighteenth Century Confronts the Gods (Cambridge, Mass.:
1959). [The Editor.]

THE DECHRISTIANIZATION OF THE
FRENCH WORKING CLASS *

Joseph N. Moody

In the long decline of mass religious belief few events played a
greater part in accelerating the process than the French Revolution.
In place of otherworldly salvation the Revolution substituted the possibility of achieving an earthly utopia where men might hope to realize
their aspirations in this life. The impact of this revolutionary myth made
itself felt on every social doctrine during the next 150 years. Consequently, the Revolution, by exchanging secular for religious goals in
the life of the masses, began a process of alienation between the French
working classes and the traditional Roman Catholic Christianity, which
had been the religion of most Frenchmen for centuries. In this regard
it has been said with more than a measure of truth that the major
missionary task of modern Christianity was not the conversion of Asian
and African peoples but the reconversion of the masses in countries
still nominally Christian. The causes of this dechristianization among
the French working classees are the subject of the following essay.

French society is a clear example of the accepted generalization
that there has been a widespread movement of the European working
class away from traditional religion. An analysis of the data does not
seem to justify a simple deterministic explanation. While it does seem
that this working class is predisposed to accept a more or less uniform approach to life, the universe, and man's relation to the absolute,

* Reprinted with the permission of the editors of Review of Politics (XX, 1958,
46–69, with omissions).

there are many historical and individual factors which modify the general attitude. Regional variations are worth further study: for instance, it is known that the area of the great abbeys, notably Burgundy, once the centers of Christian spirituality and culture, had become foci of peasant discontent and dechristianization even under the Old Regime. Workers recruited from these regions into industrial centers such as Monceau-les-Mines were religiously indifferent before they moved to the cities. Local conditions in other areas, often stemming from unfavorable land tenure, created a nascent anti-clericalism which antedates the coming of industry. The great wine producing regions of Champagne, Burgundy, the Garonne, and the Midi coast have long been weak in religious practice. These considerations make it necessary for the researcher to focus attention on the concrete circumstances in which industrialism developed. But they do not substantially alter the fact that the French working class as a whole has abandoned the faith.

In an effort to explain this phenomenon, the following considerations may be of value:

A. To a considerable degree, the traditional churches of Western Europe were outside of, and hostile to, many of the political, social and cultural currents of the nineteenth century. Partly this was the consequence of an inherent dilemma: to become effective in any age or culture, a religion must become incarnate in the concrete conditions of human life. Further, every religious faith is transmitted with a vocabulary, customs, and ceremonies adapted to the institutions and ideas of a specific culture. The success of an elaborately structured adaptation to one age is likely to become an obstacle to adjustment in rapidly changing conditions. This may explain why sudden declines in the activity of a religious body sometimes follow periods of vitality, and why there are permanent tensions within religious bodies between the "prophet" and the "priest."

During its formative period, the French working class did not find in its ancestral faith a rationale for its predicament or a meaningful source of support. To take an extreme example: Rogation Days, dutifully celebrated in all urban parishes, could not have made an immediate appeal to slum dwellers. What was needed was a new religious vocabulary, a shedding of the distinctive rural externals of religion, and an imaginative adaptation of Christian teaching to the new world of factory and railroad. It was necessary to search the religious tradition for principles that would inspire the distressed worker in his quest for justice and would support his aim for a truly human life in a degrading environment.

This would have required an acceptance of the dynamic character of the nineteenth century world. The church leaders would have had to adopt in some form the prevailing doctrine of progress, at least to the point that the new forms of production had given a new dimension to the age-old problem of poverty; and they would have had to realize that the traditional forms of charity were no longer adequate in an industrial world. Some did, and a few were even assisted in so doing by their antagonism to the newly dominant bourgeoisie. But it was a difficult task, for the Church had suffered a series of shocks in the political and intellectual realm, and the temptation was to take a total position of resistance to all that might fall under the label of the "French Revolution." Rigorous negativism rarely encourages men to grasp the objective realities of their position; in this instance it left little room, except in a valiant few, for a sympathetic approach to the workingman's position. It is instructive that a high proportion of the early social Catholics were men who had come to terms with the world in which they lived: DeCoux and Gerbert had belonged to Lamennais' *L'Avenir,* Buchez was a Saint-Simonian Socialist, Frederick Ozanam was the prototype of the Christian Democrat.

Thus the European working class was born in a century in which traditional Christianity was largely absent from the center of the stage,[1] and when the dramatic script was written in a different idiom. The new industrial proletariat did not invent its ideology, but adopted it from those, largely non-Christians, who showed themselves interested. At first, the phraseology and content of the Socialists who spoke for the workers was heavily impregnated with Christianity. Where sufficient Christian spokesmen identified themselves with the worker's cause, as in England, this condition generally continued. But where, as in France, it seemed after 1848 that the outstanding Catholics were on the side of order and property, the workers' creed became progressively anti-clerical, anti-religious, and aggressively materialistic.[2]

B. The difficulty of elaborating a Christian social doctrine that would be appealing to the industrial workers was heightened in the

[1] Professors Duroselle, Aubert, and Jemolo have sketched the exceptions in the Catholic world in *Le Liberalisme religieux au XIXième siècle, Relazione,* Tenth International Congress of Historians, Vol. V, *Storia contemporanea* (Firenze, 1956).

[2] Henri Rollet in *Sur le chantier social* (Lyon, 1955), an extension of his *l'Action sociale des catholiques de France, 1871–1901* (Paris, 1947) makes a rather good case for the rather extensive social activities, largely in the field of welfare and education, which expanded during the whole period. But these did not outweigh, in the working class mind, the unfavorable impression created by the majority of articulate Catholics.

nineteenth century by a genuine conflict between Christianity and the prevailing spirit of the time. Pierre Vermylan, Socialist member of the Belgian Senate, recently put it rather strongly:

Although behind the Socialist and Catholic program there is the same reality, and although both may attempt to satisfy the same desires, their impact on the public is different. For the basic ideas which they express are clearly distinct. The Socialists are inspired by infinite hope in human solidarity, a hope dictated as much by the heart as by reason, and by a profound confidence in man's capabilities. The Catholics, in contrast, are inclined to a humility which makes them accept servility and cling to outworn tradition.[3]

While no Catholic would accept this statement as written, it has a germ of truth. There has been a gulf between the dominant belief of the nineteenth century in the possibility of unlimited human achievement and the Christian assumption—with nuances from Thomist optimism to Jansenist and orthodox Protestant pessimism—of limited human happiness in the concrete social order.

This difference in basic approach persists in the journals and tracts read by the continental European workers. Current European working class literature indicates that the average European worker has inherited the idea structure of the eighteenth and nineteenth centuries, while the continental intellectual has largely abandoned it. The latter now writes of the tragic sense of history, of ambivalence and contingency, and of the illusions of the certainty of progress and of the rational powers of man. This may well be the origin of the *ouvrièrisme* [literally, "workerism," a term used to describe the sympathy of the French intellectual with the working class], so common in the French intellectual who admires in the worker a faith and a confidence which he himself has lost. At least, proletarian publications in France reflect little of contemporary pessimism. In writing designed for the workers, there is nothing mysterious in the world of man; all can be explained, and all could be put in order if the proper course were followed. The actual world is a broken tool, a maladjusted machine. Science could produce a world without corruption or scandal, a world of international peace and human joy—"scientism without the scientific mind," as one observer has termed it. It is this unconscious metaphysic which contributes to the working class rejection of the world it knows. Someone must be guilty, if man's aspirations have been so profoundly defeated.

[3] "Reflections on Socialism and the Catholic Church," in the *Socialist International Bulletin*, July, 1956, p. 164.

This leads, in turn, to a permanent alienation from organized society which cannot be assuaged by small gains and which nourishes the smouldering discontent which is the soil of the revolutionary spirit.

C. This revolutionary spirit is re-enforced in France by the national tradition which emphasizes the Revolution as the nodal point in French history. The average Frenchman's effective knowledge of his country's past begins with 1789. He accepts a simplified version of this central event as a triumph of good over evil, of progress over reaction. As a consequence, the popular French mind is wedded to the myth of revolution—a belief that political and social progress will come by a violent overturn of an existing system rather than by slow, evolutionary reforms. This predisposition to a revolutionary methodology, to some degree unconscious, accounts in part for the radicalism of the French working class. It has been cleverly exploited by the French Communist Party, which presents itself as the bearer of the national tradition, rather than an alien body subject to the directives of the Soviet Union.

The fact that the Revolution ultimately turned against religion and that the majority of nineteenth century Catholics rejected it radically, tended to widen the gulf between the Church and the workers. For however they might contest bourgeois political domination, the French industrial workers were sincerely devoted to the ideals of liberty and justice set forth in 1789 and could never have been enlisted in a crusade to restore the Ancien Régime. Even were they to receive active support from Conservatives who inclined to the older Conservative tradition, parallels in Britain and Germany, as well as the French experience, indicate that the workers were not to be tempted into the political camp of the Right.

A related factor in shaping the attitude of the industrial workers was the strength of the aristocratic tradition in France. The Old Regime was a massive system of special privilege, and while it disappeared in the cauldron of the Revolution, it left its impress on the bourgeoisie who inherited social and political power in the nineteenth century. The type of society in which industrialism occurs shapes in part the response of the groups affected. The introduction of industrial techniques into nineteenth century United States, which had already achieved universal manhood suffrage, an egalitarian spirit, and considerable social mobility, would necessarily produce different reactions from France where the hierarchical structure of society was more than a historic memory.

D. In addition to these general conditions, there were specific weaknesses in nineteenth century French Catholicism which contributed to the shaping of the religious attitudes of the workers:

1. The clergy were generally inadequately trained in the social sciences for the serious tasks of the century. The French hierarchy was able to rebuild the physical plant of the seminaries after the disaster of the Revolution, but they never succeeded in raising the level of clerical education to that of the eighteenth century. The training was particularly defective in fields which would have promoted an understanding of the rapidly evolving conditions in French society.

2. The tradition of social distance between the clergy and people persisted. In rural regions this would evoke little comment. Nor would the bourgeoisie resent it, for they were preoccupied with their own status and affairs. But the working class emphasis on comradeship and solidarity was foreign to the traditional relationship of clergy and people.

3. The bulk of the clergy were allied with the parties of the political Right, the *"alliance du sabre et du goupillon"* [loosely translated as the "alliance of the sword and the holy water font"]. This was particularly decisive after 1848 when the workers' swing to republicanism was accompanied by a sharp intensification in proletarian anti-clericalism. At the same time there was begun that hesitant and gradual return of many of the bourgeoisie to the practice of religion, a movement summarized in the classic, "The sons of Voltaire became the sons of the Church." While always partial, it was sufficient to create a class identification with religious practice that has had tremendous effects on working class attitudes.

4. The loss of revenue-producing properties in the Revolution forced the clergy to greater dependence on the wealthy, while it handicapped some welfare activities. The poverty of the modern French Church may have been a long-range blessing, but it has unfavorable side effects.

5. The failure to build new churches in fast growing industrial suburbs. There is no more striking sight in the environs of Paris and other French cities than the little church, intended for a village, and now serving a sprawling urban area. In addition to being inadequate, it is often away from the main current of the new life which has engulfed it. Nor does it provide those human services which once made it a social center of primary interest, for parish structures and spirit remained anachronistic.

6. The stand taken by lay Christian leaders on concrete social issues convinced the workers that religion was not concerned with their conditions. Silence on necessary reforms also aroused hostility. When workers found political parties, to which Christians belonged, uninterested

in their plight, they concluded that religion was allied to the existing social order and to political resistance to reform.

E. All recent studies in the field of religious sociology agree that social structures and conditions are a vital element in religious practice. These social factors operate indirectly, gradually (rarely are there wholesale defections, and the elite go first), and progressively, with a minimum of success in reversing the tide. There are always exceptions where convictions are strong. The impact of social factors is greatest in areas where the religious framework is closely integrated with the social, and less in regions of divided religious adherence.

A prime social factor is the industrial city itself. A church could play a vital role in village social life where all human activity is geographically concentrated. In a city all is movement and mobility: residence is often changed, especially among the poorer classes; work and leisure are often far from home. As Louis Wirth wrote: in a great city most men spend a great part of their time travelling from a place where they do not wish to live to another where they would prefer not to work. With the occupational and residential fluidity, there is a greater complexity of economic function, and a corresponding heterogeneity of social classes, which tend to become fixed in separate zones or residential quarters.

The character of personal relations is also changed by urbanization. "Physical contacts are close, but social contacts are distant." The clergy are no longer in close touch with their people, and face to face contacts are superficial. The influence of the clergy is lessened as its activities before functional. There is also a considerable impact on the new arrivals from the country who find the natural rhythm of the village replaced by the artificial and accelerated pace of urban life—from waltz to bebop, as one observer described it.

It is with these *déracinées* [persons alienated from their native surroundings] that the rupture with religious practice was most sharp. The old saw that the Breton peasant checks his faith in the Gare de Montparnasse has general validity.[4] Where religious practice is closely associated with a social milieu, the transplanting itself is enough to destroy it.

[4] For a study of the Breton emigration and its religious effects, cf. Elie Gautier, *La Dure existence des paysans et paysannes* (Paris, 1950); *L'Émigration bretonne,* Bulletin de l'entraide bretonne de la region parisienne, Paris, (n.d.); *La Vie morale et religieuse des bretons émigrés* (Paris, Sept. 1954). For the whole problem, cf. Robert Kothen, *L'Église et les mouvements de population* (Bruxelles, 1945).

The technical changes of the industrial period effected an uprooting in time for the artisans already living in the towns; for the peasant émigrés, it has been one in time and in space. It was so profound an uprooting that the word "revolution" hardly describes it. It may be best considered as a brusque mutation, something similar to the impact of Western culture on the backward regions in our time.

A number of factors intensified the unfavorable consequences of environmental changes:

1. The ultimate destruction of the *confréries, compagnonnages,* and similar workingmen's associations, eliminated institutions which bound artisans to religion in the pre-industrial period.

2. The acute misery of the *déracinées* in the early phases of industrialization was highly unfavorable to religious practice. The naked struggle for survival, the disruption of family life, child and female labor, miserable housing, and the lack of wholesome leisure all conspired to destroy interest in spiritual values or in the concept of a religion of love.[5] Once the pattern was set, alienation from religious practice became traditional among the industrial workers.

3. The class consciousness which resulted from these conditions and the feeling of solidarity with fellow sufferers contributed to an acute hostility toward the "others" who were seen as the source of the injustice. It became accepted without question that men and machines alike served the owners, with the workers condemned to an unreasonable austerity. The assumption of superiority on the part of the managers hardened the resentment and suspicion. In some the response reached revolutionary intensity: these were *les hommes debout,* the men of action and struggle; in others there was merely a dull sense of hurt.

Once this attitude of collective discontent was fixed, it was impervious to statistical evidence that the standard of living of the French worker was slowly rising in the nineteenth century. Nor was it improved by contact with management. A non-Communist official of the CGT has described a meeting of a *comité d'enterprise* in a metal factory in a Parisian suburb. The meeting is required by law, but was purely perfunctory. The workers' delegates filed into the panelled room first and waited uneasily, feeling out of place in their blouses and blues. The managers entered with their staff and briefcases, anxious to keep the proceedings to a minimum and to get back to serious work. The

---

[5] For details, cf. Edouard Dolleans, *Histoire du mouvement ouvrier,* III Tomes, (Paris, 1936–1953); Georges Duveau, *La Vie ouvrière en France sous le Second Empire* (Paris, 1946); for a current fictionalized account, cf. Henri Lespes, *L'Usine sans âme* (Paris, 1954).

workers stared across the table at the white hand and neat clothes of their opposite numbers. A report was hurriedly read, questions parried with generalities, and demands casually dismissed. Some of the workers' delegates read newspapers during the proceedings to show their disdain. Two hours of futility passed with cool defiance on both sides.

This feeling of class is so keenly felt that it can be projected into other areas. The same author gives an amusing story of a young female worker who had been a patient in a nuns' hospital and had described her experience in terms of class struggle. The young sisters in the ward were nice and were overburdened with work. They were trying at the same time to pass their nurses' exam. The "boss" nun not only exploited them as any other *patron,* but did her best to see that they did not pass the examination. Her guilt was obvious, for she consorted with the well-to-do, while the young sisters worked with the poor patients.

Contact with the working class in France, and in other continental areas, would convince the observer that these attitudes precede an acceptance of Marxism. So well prepared is the soil for the message that rarely is serious argument or extensive reading necessary for conversion. Once heard, revolutionary Marxism appeals to the workers' sense of hurt; and it seems to come closest to his aspirations for it promises what he seeks. He is buoyed by the vision of the march of history and is intrigued by the concept of the dying phase of capitalism. Such a worthy cause merits full faith and generous sacrifice. He is not disturbed by conflicting reports of life behind the Iron Curtain. He knows little of the objective reality, and creates a picture to fit his dreams. He dismisses contrary evidence, since it comes from the enemy. Immured in a closed world, "he camps at the gate of the nation," in Auguste Comte's phrase, awaiting the day of deliverance. If he thinks of Christianity at all, he would declare it so betrayed by its adherents that he—a worker—must seek another faith.

This revolutionary *mystique,* rooted in many segments of the European proletariat, is obviously incompatible with the traditional religions of the West. When added to the workers' conviction that religious practice is identical with bourgeois status, there is created "the wall" separating the Church from the world of the worker.

BIBLIOGRAPHY

Adrian Dansette, *Religious History of Modern France* (2 vols.; New York: 1961). Michael P. Fogarty, *Christian Democracy in Western Europe, 1820–1953* (Notre Dame, Ind.: 1957). K. S. Inglis, *Churches and the Working Class in Victorian England* (London: 1963). General works covering this and succeeding sections: Paul Droulers, S. J., "Le catholicisme dans le monde aux XIXᵉ siècle," *Journal of World History*, V (1959–60), 375–401. E. E. Y. Hales, *The Catholic Church in the Modern World* (Garden City, N.Y.: 1961). J. Katz, "Jewry and Judaism in the Nineteenth Century," *Journal of World History*, IV (1958), 881–900. Kenneth S. Latourette, *Christianity in a Revolutionary Age: A History of Christianity in the Nineteenth and Twentieth Centuries* (5 vols.; New York: 1958–62). James MacCaffrey, *History of the Catholic Church in the Nineteenth Century* (2nd ed.; St. Louis: 1910). Herbert Schneider, "The Developments in Protestantism during the Nineteenth Century throughout the World," *Journal of World History*, VI (1960–61), 97–119. [The Editor.]

THE SOCIAL GOSPEL *

Alan H. Hamilton

The increasingly wider acceptance of a secularized world view during the nineteenth century had a serious effect upon the various Christian denominations. With the industrialization of the West, the growth of what came to be known as "social conscience," the slow but marked rise in living standards in many societies, and, finally but perhaps most significantly, with the spread of socialism and other reform movements, the pressure on the established religious faiths to apply the teachings of Scripture directly to the solution of social problems became too strong to resist. There was danger, in fact, that if they did not do so they might cease to have any moral authority in human affairs. Perhaps, because of its greater diversity and the larger measure of lay control in its churches, the various branches of Protestantism responded earlier than the Catholic Church to these demands. The important and often very direct influence of socialism in its several forms had much to do with the rise of the "Social Gospel" within Protestantism. Here we learn something of the way in which the ideas of the socialist movement influenced Protestant Christianity.

The concept of socialism has historically gathered within its borders numerous elements which make it hard of definition. A date for

---

* Reprinted with the permission of the editors of *Bibliotheca Sacra* (CVIII, No. 429, January–March, 1951, 81–97, with omissions).

the beginning of socialism will depend upon our definition of the movement. Oscar Jaszi outlines six characteristics which have been found common to all the varying ideologies in its history as well as to the more definitely organized developments of the post-Renaissance period. Says he "these are: first, a condemnation of the existing political and social order as unjust; second, an advocacy of a new order consistent with moral values; third, a belief that this ideal is realizable; fourth, a conviction that the immorality of the established order is traceable not to a fixed world-order or to the unchanging nature of man, but to corrupt institutions; fifth, a program of action leading to the ideal through a fundamental remolding of human nature or of institutions or both; and sixth, a revolutionary will to carry out this program."

The affinity of the social gospel movement for a program containing these principles is immediately evident. It is further substantiated by the fact that movements identified as socialistic prior to the 18th century were associated with religious, or at least strongly idealistic, concepts. . . .

Socialism of the modern type, however, is inextricably linked with the rise of the capitalistic system. Something of its rise has been noticed already. It may be helpful at this point to see the system through the eyes of a Socialist of the modern type. Sidney and Beatrice Webb describe it as "the particular stage in the development of industry and legal institutions in which the bulk of the workers find themselves divorced from the ownership of the instruments of production, in such a way as to pass into the position of wage-earners whose subsistence, security and personal freedom seem dependent on the will of a relatively small proportion of the nation, namely, those who own—and through their legal ownership control—the organization of the land, the machinery and the labor force of the community; and do so with the object of making for themselves individual and private gain." [1]

In the same year in which Marx and Engels produced a *Communist Manifesto* and a number of years before its principles actually attained wide acceptance, a group known as the Christian Socialists was formed in England. Its accepted leader was a clergyman, Frederick Denison Maurice, back of whom lay the influences of Fourier and the Chartist movement. The last-mentioned movement is thought to be one of the first efforts of the proletariat to organize for the gaining of political power; and it was at one of their meetings, held in a tense atmosphere that augured violence, that the initial step of the Christian Socialist program was motivated. In the meeting were Rev. Charles Kingsley, an

[1] *The Decay of Capitalist Civilization*, pp. x–xi.

associate of Maurice in the Anglican church, and John Ludlow, a young barrister who had brought the influence of Fourier to bear upon both of these ministers. Believing that the Chartist movement was doomed to failure and unnecessary bloodshed because it lacked the religious ideal, these men spent the night preparing placards which appeared next morning over the city of London. Each one addressed to "the workmen of England" and signed "a working parson," they brought the assurance that "the Almighty God and Jesus Christ, the poor Man who died for poor men, will bring freedom for you, though all the Mammonites on earth were against you."

The ministers and laymen who formed this band of Christian Socialists cannot apparently be thought of as reformers whose alliance with the church was rather insignificant. It is recorded of them, on the contrary, that their weekly Bible reading as a group was "the sacrament of their unity, the means whereby they received their inspiration." Such concern as they did show at this point, however, was based upon the fact that "they found the church—to which they were passionately attached—accepting and even commending the views of philosophers, politicians and economists whose knowledge of public questions it reckoned superior to its own. . . . The Christian Socialists challenged both the validity of this teaching and the right of the church to identify itself therewith." It is of interest, then, to notice that nearly one century later a German sociologist stood before another group of English clergymen and gave the following challenge and diagnosis: "With the coming of the Renaissance and liberalism, Christianity failed to remain the basic ferment and integrating force in social life. The main consequences of this failure deserve attention. (1) The spiritualization and regulation of human affairs, public and private, has gradually been left to the competing institutions in society—to family, community, business, trade unions, parties, army, public opinion and its exponents, press, wireless, cinema, associations, age groups, groups of intelligentsia, clubs, etc. . . . (2) Of course, the withdrawal of the Christian churches from the main zones of social life was not complete: wherever they maintained their hold on tradition and influenced the ways of life, their impact was very considerable. But wherever they lost touch with the concrete, topical issues of social life, this immediately reacted upon them by increasing formalism and reducing religion to an affair of attending Sunday sermons. . . . (3) To this loss of a foothold in society at large by the churches very often corresponded a readiness on the part of their leaders to cooperate with the ruling classes, and to identify themselves with their vested interests both in

a spiritual and a material sense. . . . (4) This close association between conservatism, or even reaction, and the church contributed a
great deal in its turn to the prevailing distrust felt by the public regarding most of the proposals coming from the church, to give a lead to
social change and organization." [2]

The main attempt of these early Christian Socialists to put their
convictions into action took the form of a cooperative effort in production. Though such effort was ultimately to fail, it is generally conceded
the movement had a measure of success in convincing the rising proletariat that the church had a definite concern for its problems. Perhaps
the most potent of the agencies for making the new organization known
was the short-lived periodical the Christian Socialist, which was edited
by Ludlow.

In one of the early issues of his journal Ludlow wrote: "A new idea
has gone abroad into the world—that socialism, the latest born of the
forces now at work in modern society, and Christianity, the eldest born
of those forces, are in their nature not hostile but akin to each other; or
rather that the one is but the development, the outgrowth, the manifestation of the other. . . . That Christianity, however feeble and torpid
it may seem to many just now, is truly but as an eagle at moult; that
socialism is but its livery of the 19th century which it is even now
putting on, to spread erelong its wings for a broader and heavenlier
flight. That socialism without Christianity, on the one hand, was life-
less as the feathers without the bird—however skillfully the stuffer may
dress them up into an artificial semblance of life. That every socialist
system which has maintained itself has stood upon the moral grounds
of righteousness, self-sacrifice, mutual affection and common brother-
hood. . . . That Christianity, on the other hand, in this 19th century
of ours becomes in its turn chilly and helpless when stripped of its
social influences; or, in other words, when divorced from socialism." [3]

That Ludlow and his associates were thinking not merely of the
extending of Christian influences to society by the presence of individual Christians within society, but of a thoroughgoing application to
the economic and political structure of principles believed to have their
rootage in the Christian faith—thus sharing a common objective with
all socialism—must be kept in mind. The Christian Socialists of that
early day, though they could be criticized for a naïve simplification of
the economic problem, were true socialists. In the editorial by Ludlow
just cited, for example, he goes on to say: "If the gospel speaks true and

[2] Karl Mannheim, *Diagnosis of Our Times,* pp. 109–11.
[3] Cf. Bliss, *Encyclopedia of Social Reform,* p. 252.

ye 'cannot serve God and mammon,' it is wholly incompatible with a political economy which proclaims self-interest to be the very pivot of social action . . . . but it is compatible with those theories or systems which have for a common object to bind up into fellowship, and not to divide by selfishness and rivalry; to substitute fair prices and living wages for a false cheapness and starvation, its child; and which have adopted for their watchwords Association and Exchange instead of Competition and Profit. . . . If it be given us to vindicate for Christianity its true authority over the realms of industry and trade, for socialism its true character as the great Christian revolution of the 19th century, so that the title of socialist shall be only a bugbear to the idle and to the wicked, and society from the highest rank to the lowest shall avowedly regulate itself upon the principle of cooperation and not drift rudderless upon the sea of competition, as our let-alone political economists would have it do—then indeed we shall have achieved our task."

Two movements worthy of note followed afterwards in the train of the Christian Socialists. One—the Guild of St. Matthew—was an Anglo-Catholic undertaking founded by Steward Headlam in 1877 but hindered by its extreme ecclesiasticism from continuing. The other was the more conservative Christian Social Union formed in England by 1889, having the great scholar of New Testament Greek, Brooke Foss Westcott, for president. In its principles were stated the following three objectives: to claim for the Christian law ultimate authority to rule social practice; to study in common how to apply the moral truth and principles of Christianity to the social and economic difficulties of the present time; to present Christ in practical life as the living Master and King, the enemy of wrong and selfishness, the power of righteousness and love.[4]

Two years before formation of the Union Westcott had published his volume *Social Aspects of Christianity* and in the preface made an acknowledgment to four writers whose works had done much to mold his own social thought as a Christian. All four of them reveal additional roots for social Christianity, but they can have no more than mention in a brief review such as may be found here. One of the men was Brewer, whose introduction to Dugdale's *Monumenta Franciscana* had stirred up Westcott's interest in the social conditions of Europe prevailing at the time that the Franciscan order began. Another was Clarkson; he and Canon Curteis had served to depict forcefully the social activity of the Quakers who had been active in social melioration from the beginning of the movement (as far back as 1647). A third was

[4] Cf. Bliss, *op. cit.*, p. 260.

Comte, in whose *Politique Positive* Westcott claims to have found "a powerful expression of many salient features of that which I had long held to be the true social embodiment of the gospel—of a social ideal which the faith in Christ is alone, I believe, able to realise." [5] The fourth was Maurice himself of whose book *Social Morality* Westcott says, "Few books can teach nobler lessons."

Although the Christian Social Union did not commit itself to any one school of economic thought it was not hesitant in declaring that the then present order was wrong. The chairman of its London branch Canon H. Scott Holland, in the tract *The Ground of Our Appeal,* pleads that there must be those within the church who will give themselves to a thorough study of the social, economic and political situation, and then offer the church instruction in the steps it must take to apply Christian principles to the needs. These trained Christian investigators, said Hollland, will "arrive at the discussion possessed by two deep convictions: first, that the present situation is intolerable; and second, that its solution must be found in the unfaltering assertion of moral—as supreme over mechanical—laws. . . . It is to collect together such men as this, it is to foster and to enlarge such a spirit that the Christian Social Union exists." [6]

Other countries also had their Christian leaders who were stirred into social action by the conditions on every side. France, Germany and Belgium had their Christian Socialists, but it was the English movement that was to add another significant element to the background of the social gospel effort. In 1891 an affiliate Christian Social Union was formed in the United States among ministers of the Protestant Episcopal church, which was to become an outstanding agency of its time as an educative factor in the developing social Christianity of America. Among its 100 publications were pamphlets written by the English leaders Bishop Westcott and Canon Gore, emphasizing particularly the social significance of two doctrines—those of the incarnation and the church.

This picture of socialism as a background for the social gospel movement would not be complete without mention of the synthesis of socialist thought known as Marxian socialism. In the popular mind, Karl Marx and all that he stood for are totally divorced from Christianity. But Latourette writes: "Even Marx was probably under more obligation to the Jewish-Christian tradition than he quite realized. Of Jewish blood, on both his father's and his mother's side he was descended from

---

[5] *Social Aspects of Christianity,* p. xii.
[6] Cf. Bliss, *op. cit.,* p. 261.

a long line of rabbis. His father became a Protestant Christian while Karl was a child—probably to escape from the narrow bonds of Jewish intellectual life into the freedom offered by the liberal Protestantism with which he was acquainted. Marx owed much to Hegel who, in turn, was deeply indebted to Christianity. . . . Marx, too, came in touch with a marked revival movement in Christianity. His wife's half-sister was caught up actively in it. Moreover, Marx—like 19th century socialists in general—assumed a view of history which had as its essence a millenarianism, a belief in the progress of society towards a golden age, which was almost certainly the result of the long impregnation of the thought of Europe with Jewish-Christian teaching. It was primarily from Judaism and Christianity that the conviction of the perfectibility of human society was derived."

BIBLIOGRAPHY

Paul A. Carter, *The Decline and Revival of the Social Gospel* (Ithaca, N.Y.: 1956). Torben Christensen, *Origin and History of Christian Socialism, 1848–54* (Aarhus, Denmark: 1962). Leonard Elliott-Binns, *Religion of the Victorian Era* (London: 1936). Robert T. Handy, "Christianity and Socialism in America, 1900–1920," *Church History*, XXI (1952), 39–54. Charles H. Hopkins, *The Rise of the Social Gospel in American Protestantism, 1865–1915* (New Haven: 1937, 1961). Arthur M. Ramsay, *F. D. Maurice and the Conflicts of Modern Theology* (Cambridge, Eng.: 1951). Guy H. Ransom, "The Kingdom of God as the Design of Society: F. D. Maurice," *Church History*, XXX (1961), 458–472. [The Editor.]

LEO XIII: TWO CONCEPTS OF GOVERNMENT *

John Courtney Murray, S.J.

The growing pressures of nineteenth-century secularism were stoutly resisted by the Roman Catholic Church during most of the century. Such resistance created a dilemma. Secularism might endanger the

---

* Reprinted with the permission of Rev. John Courtney Murray, S.J., President, Theological Studies, Inc. (*Theological Studies*, XIV, 1953, 551–567, with omissions).

*soul's salvation, but powerful secular movements like socialism and lib-
eralism promised men a solution to their mundane problems. The appeal of these doctrines could hardly be resisted by masses of human
beings who saw in them a means of alleviating human misery in their
present lives. For that reason the various encyclicals and pronounce-
ments of Pope Pius IX (1846–78), who sensed the dangerous implications of secularism, sometimes made it appear that the Church as an
institution was permanently allied with the forces of political conservatism. The task of reemphasizing the Church's concern for human welfare was undertaken by Pope Leo XIII (1878–1903), whose encyclical
Rerum novarum issued in 1891 placed the Church squarely on the side
of social justice. In essence, Pope Leo rejected both unbridled liberalism
and socialism but stated a moral charge that the state and society had
an obligation to look after the welfare of the masses. The state should
become neither the instrument of a socialist monolith, nor should it be
completely indifferent to human welfare as the teachings of laissez-faire
liberalism seemed to imply. The nature of this important distinction in
Pope Leo's social thought is the theme of Father Murray's discussion in
the essay that follows.*

As the Social Question pressed more and more urgently upon the
Christian conscience in the latter half of the nineteenth century, two
general schools of thought developed in Catholic circles with regard to
the role of government in its solution. In Germany, where discussion
was most active, the so-called Minimists came to be led by Bishop Frep-
pel. The other school, the so-called Interventionists, came under the
more vigorous leadership of Bishop Ketteler. When Leo XIII finally
issued *Rerum novarum* in 1891, he firmly took his stand with Ketteler.
This was a bold move, not pleasing to many Catholics. But when the
initial resistance had been dissipated, the move was seen to be provi-
dential. By it, as someone has remarked, Leo XIII took the revolutionary
flavor out of a strong program of government intervention in the socio-
economic order; this was a necessary step toward the solution of the
Social Question. In our day the four classic texts are almost too well
known to need quotation.

First, *Rerum novarum* assigns to government a "general providence"
over society. The broad principle is stated in this pregnant, if not altogether clear, sentence: "Those who are in power ought chiefly to give
their assistance in general and all along the line, by the whole pattern
of laws and institutions; in other words, they ought to bring it about

that the prosperity both of the community and of private individuals may grow spontaneously out of the very structure and administration of the state." [1] This broad principle is the general premise of possible intervention by government in the socio-economic order.

The second classic text states the conditions and limits of this governmental intervention: "If therefore any injury has been done, or threatens to be done to the interests of the community (*rebus communibus*)—the kind of injury which cannot otherwise be repaired or prevented—it is necessary for public authority to intervene." [2] There follows an enumeration of the properly social kind of disorders which call for governmental action. The text then goes on: "In all these cases the force and authority of law obviously ought to be employed, within certain limits. And these limits are determined by the same principle which demands the aid of law—the principle, namely, that the law ought not to undertake more, nor ought it to go farther, than the remedy of evils or the removal of danger requires." [3] This text makes clear that governmental intervention is hypothetical, per accidens, ad hoc.

A third classic text states the essential action required of government; it is action, not properly intervention. It is an action in favor of those free associations within the commonwealth upon which, according to the principles of right social order, there falls in the first instance the responsibility for promoting the particular social goods which integrate the common good: "Let the state protect these lawfully associated bodies of citizens; but let it not intrude into their internal affairs and order of life; for vital activity is set in motion by an interior principle, and it is very easily shattered by outside interference." [4] This principle struck at the social theory and polity, individualist in philosophical origin and totalitarian in political tendency, which denied and destroyed all intermediary institutions between the individual and the state.

The final classic text concerns the special duty of government to come to the aid of the "unhappy multitude, which has no security through resources of its own" (*miserum vulgus, nullis opibus suis tutum*).[5] Leo XIII has specially in view the growing urban proletariat, the new social phenomenon brought forth by the Industrial Revolu-

---

[1] *Two Basic Social Encyclicals* (Washington: Catholic University Press, 1943), *Rerum novarum*, n. 48, p. 40; here and elsewhere I have emended the translation.
[2] *Ibid.*, n. 52, p. 47.
[3] *Ibid.*, n. 53, p. 48.
[4] *Ibid.*, n. 75, p. 72.
[5] *Ibid.*, n. 54, p. 48; cf. n. 49, p. 42.

tion. Not absent from his view, however, was the age-old peasant, who had long been a characteristic of the European scene. This text, therefore, takes account of actually prevalent conditions of social disorder.

All these principles received greater clarification and development as later thinkers reflected on the experience of developing industrial society. The fruit of their reflection was codified in *Quadragesimo anno*, which goes beyond the argument of *Rerum novarum*, especially in what concerns the principle of subsidiary function, the freedom of the various "orders" in society, and the generic duty of the political authority to aid in elaborating the structure of society, principally by aiding the growth of free socio-economic associations.[6] These further developments need not be brought into view here; they are substantially in the line set by Leo XIII when he defined the relation of government to the social and economic order.

A less well known text may be quoted in conclusion; it is found in an allocution to a group of French workers, delivered in 1887. After recalling the past services of the Church to the poor and to the workers, "not only by largesse of charity, but by creating and encouraging those great corporative institutions which contributed so powerfully to the progress of the arts and crafts" as well as to the security of the worker, the Pope states this principle with regard to the socio-economic function of government:

Without a doubt, the intervention and action of these (public) powers are not indispensably necessary, when conditions in labor and industry reveal nothing which offends against morality, justice, human dignity, the domestic life of the worker. But when any of these values is menaced or compromised, the public powers, intervening in proper fashion and in just measure, are to do a work of social salvation; for it falls to their charge to protect and safeguard the true interests of the citizens under their obedience.[7]

These texts assign to government a properly political task with regard to the socio-economic order. It is a political task, first, because it is prompted by the exigencies of properly social goods—the particular social goods of various groups as well as the general welfare as such. Political

---

[6] No proper English equivalent has yet been found for the Latin, "ordines" and "collegia ordinum," of Pius XI. Tentatively, the terms "industry councils" and "industry council plan" have been adopted; cf. John F. Cronin, *Catholic Social Principles* (Milwaukee: Bruce, 1950), pp. 221–22.

[7] Allocution, *Grande est la joie* (Oct. 18, 1887), Desclée, III, 14.

power does not act in the personal interests of the private individual as such.[8] The task is political, secondly, because it is strictly limited; all political tasks as limited. The general principle of limitation is again the common good, as a whole or in its constituent parts. Concretely, the leading principle of limitation is the rightful and necessary freedom of society in all its associational forms to direct and govern itself, under the "general providence" of government. The freedom of society is an essential element of the common good; for in society, and not in government, reside the vital energies which make for public prosperity.

Consequently, the first criterion of governmental intervention is necessity—the necessity created by the fact that important human values are being damaged or menaced. Moreover, the damage must be substantive; the menace must be grave. Both must assume the proportions of a social evil. Furthermore, resort to government must be in the nature of a last resort; the damage must be irremediable, the danger irremovable, by any other agency. Again, as it is prompted by necessity, so governmental intervention must not be pushed beyond the limits of necessity: ". . . the law ought not to undertake more, nor ought it to go farther, than the remedy of evils or the removal of danger requires." Governmental action looks primarily to the restoration of an order of freedom; when this order is established, the free forces within the order again resume their rightful role.

Finally, governmental action is limited by its mode, which is the political mode of law. Law is a necessary instrument of social order; its value, in fact, is measured by its necessity. However, its value is limited, even if it be regarded as a directive force, and still more limited if it be regarded as a coercive force. The more important forces that make for social order rise from the depths of the free human spirit—the forces of civic virtue, which gives birth to a love of the common good and to a spirit of voluntary cooperation towards its achievement; the forces of moral virtue, which instil a spirit of social justice and charity into all human associations; and above all the forces of religious faith, which are ultimately the ordering forces of all human life, social as well as individual.

This is the place to note the purely relative value that Leo XIII puts on human civil law and its directive and coercive force as a means towards social order. It is at times a necessary means, but always of

<hr>

[8] "Since law of its nature envisages the common good, it would do wrong to concern itself with singular and rare cases; there is no need to fear that such cases would trouble that peace and tranquillity which is the proper end of political authority" (Bonne Presse, III, 180).

itself an insufficient one. Texts in this sense abound; the following are typical. In the Encyclical, *Diuturnum,* after speaking of the dangers of communism, socialism, and nihilism, the Pope continues:

The more serious thing is that in the midst of these great dangers civil rulers do not have at their disposal sufficiently adequate means whereby public order may be restored and peace established among men. They arm themselves with the authority of laws; they think to coerce by the severity of punishments those who are disturbing society. This is right enough. But what needs serious consideration is the fact that the force of punishment can never be so great as of itself to preserve public order. Fear, as St. Thomas says, is a 'weak foundation'. . . . One must make up one's mind that not even the severity of laws can be fruitful, unless men are moved by a sense of duty, and animated by a salutary fear of God.[9]

In the Encyclical, *Exeunte iam anno,* the ultimate premise of the inadequacy of human law as a redemptive force is laid down: man's redemption is ultimately found only in Christ:

Wherefore those who are endeavoring to extinguish the rising flames of passion among the populace by turning the force of law against them are indeed acting in the cause of justice. But let them understand that they will spend their labor with little or no result as long as they are obstinately determined to reject the virtue of the Gospel and to refuse the proffered assistance of the Church. The remedy for social evils lies in a change of heart, in a private and public return to Jesus Christ and to the Christian way of life.[10]

One last text may be quoted from the Allocution, *Il y a deux ans:*

It behooves those who hold civil power to be penetrated with this truth, that, in order to dispel the danger that threatens society, neither human laws, nor repressions by magistrates, nor the arms of soldiers will be sufficient. What is above all else important, indeed indispensable, is that the Church should be afforded freedom to recall to men's mind the commands of God and to extend her saving influence throughout all classes of society.[11]

In the context of this question—the value of law in society—there recurs Leo XIII's endless, insistent theme, the necessity of religion in society, and to this end, the freedom of the Church. These texts needed to be cited for the sake of perspective; Leo XIII sets value on law, but he

---

[9] Encyclical, *Diuturnum* (June 29, 1881), Desclée, I, 231.
[10] Encyclical, *Exeunte iam anno* (Dec. 4, 1888), Desclée, III, 194.
[11] Allocution, *Il y a deux ans* (Oct. 30, 1889), Desclée, III, 283.

regarded its value as secondary to conditions of religious and moral health in society. Law is not the main cause of these conditions; indeed, it is effective in proportion as it is the manifestation of their existence. Whether Leo XIII was always fully faithful to this minimist concept of the value of law, especially when he touches the matter of the role of government in the religio-cultural order, is a question later to be discussed. In any event, he was not on principle a protagonist of the theory that would build society from the top down, by law. The good society will be good by reason of the creative and constructive forces of virtue active in its depths. At best, law can only protect and direct these vital forces.

What impressed his contemporaries, and dismayed some of them, was his firm theory of governmental interventionism, in the socio-economic order. The surprise and dismay were natural in the heyday of laisser-faire and of the "umpire state." What impresses us, on the contrary, in our age of totalitarianisms of the right and of the left, is the Pope's concern to set careful limits to governmental intervention. Part of this concern derived from the presence on the scene of an Enemy, European doctrinaire socialism in its various forms, verging from left to extreme left. But the main concern was to hew to the line of sound political principles. Leo XIII boldly took from the Enemy the truth that he had—the principle that government, under the conditions of modern society, must take an active role in economic life. In grasping this problem the United States, in the person of Andrew Jackson, was nearly six decades ahead of *Rerum novarum*. Industrialism had wrought a progressive depersonalization of economic life. And the impersonality of the employer-employee relationship had in turn bred moral irresponsibility. A new "master" had appeared, the corporation. And, as the American aphorism had it, "Corporations have neither bodies to be kicked nor souls to be damned." They were seemingly immune from the restraints that conscience had imposed on the old "master," the individual, in an age when economic relationships were generally personal. The private conscience had ceased to be an effective means of social control. Therefore the only alternative to the tyranny of socialism or the anarchy of economic liberalism was the growth of the public conscience and its expression through the medium of law and governmental act—a medium whose impersonality matched the impersonality of the economic life into which it was thrust as a principle of order. On these grounds Leo XIII took his stand for interventionism. At the same time he brought the whole weight of his teaching office to bear on the more fundamental problem, the education

of the public conscience. In this latter connection one rarely cited text
is pertinent. It is sometimes said that Leo XIII gave too much attention to the *principes,* to the men who actually held the power of rule,
and too little attention to the people, to the development of their
capacity for self-rule. There is some ground for this charge; for it is
a charge. However, the following text sets the perspectives more
exactly:

> It is recorded in our memory of blessed Father Francis and of his most
> distinguished disciples that they were men dedicated to the people and
> accustomed to devote their efforts with consuming diligence to the public
> good. Look around you now at men and at affairs. Surely you will see
> that it is time for you to take up again that same plan of life, and coura-
> geously imitate the example of those men of old. Certainly in this day,
> more than ever before, the well-being of society depends to a great extent
> upon the people. It is therefore the duty of both orders of clerics to know
> the multitude at first hand, and to come with love to its aid, teaching,
> admonishing, comforting; for the multitude not only bears the frequent
> burden of poverty and hard work but is also beset with snares and dangers.
> Indeed, if We ourselves have written letters to the bishops about the Masonic
> sect, about the conditions of the working man, about the chief duties of
> Christian citizens, and about kindred subjects, we have written these
> letters chiefly for the sake of the people, that they may learn from them
> to estimate their rights and duties, to look out for themselves, and to will
> that proper provision be made for their welfare.[12]

There is in this text the germ of a great idea, which Leo XIII certainly glimpsed, even though he did not fully elaborate it. I mean the
idea that the people are responsible for their own temporal destinies,
that the well-being of society depends largely on them, that powerful
dynamisms of political and social change are resident in a people
which has estimated its rights and duties in a Christian sense and is
determined that the popular will, formed by this estimate, should be
represented when the structures of society are shaped and the direction of its movement decided upon.

At the time (1898) this idea had, of course, gone far beyond the
germinal stage in the United States; behind it already lay some three
centuries of growth—a growth so burgeoning as to evidence some
rankness. In this sense one may perhaps feel that the Pope came rather
belatedly upon the idea. In any event, within the religio-political culture of the so-called Catholic nations, in which long centuries of absolutism—royal, confessional, enlightened, Liberal—(and, one might

[12] Letter to the General of the Order of Friars Minor.

add, equally long centuries of a "religion of the state") had left as their inheritance the Catholic masses, passive with regard to their social fate as well as indifferent to their Christian faith, the idea was hardly more than germinal.

This brief digression to Leo XIII's efforts to foster the seed of the future was made for the sake of perspective. In returning to his political concept of government, the next thing to be noted is the way he effectively dethroned the principle which he took from the Enemy on the left—the principle of interventionism—from the status it had in the Enemy's camp, the status of an absolute. Governmental intervention is not an absolute, any more than "free enterprise" (as the Enemy on the right understood the term) is an absolute. Intervention is relative to the proved social damage or danger consequent on social imbalance and disorder. At the same time, Leo XIII was not captive to the doctrinairism latent in the pseudo-axiom, "That government governs best which governs least." He actually took the ground from under the later argument, which was pitched on a sort of quantitative statement of the question: Is there "too much" government? That is not the question. Rather, the question in Leo XIII's mind was: Is government promoting "too much" or "too little" the interests of a particular class or group?

Leo XIII's relativist and realist concept of the political role of government in economic and social life preserves him from the doctrinairism of both the Right and the Left. It reveals a healthy distrust of government when it begins to infringe upon the freedom of society and its natural and free associational forms. At the same time it reveals a sound respect for government when it acts within the limits of social necessities created by irresponsible uses or abuses of freedom.

BIBLIOGRAPHY

Edward T. Gargan (ed.), *Leo XIII and the Modern World* (New York: 1961). E. E. Y. Hales, *Pio Nono: a Study in European Politics and Religion in the Nineteenth Century* (2nd ed.; London: 1956); *Revolution and Papacy, 1769–1846* (New York: 1960). Eduardo Soderini, *The Pontificate of Leo XIII* (London: 1934). [The Editor.]

FROM SECULARISM TO HUMANISM:
AN ASPECT OF VICTORIAN THOUGHT *

John Gillard Watson

With the weakening of mass religious belief one of the great concerns of many western secular thinkers was the reconstruction of a system of ethics completely divorced from the traditional theism of Christianity and Judaism. The first widespread effort in this direction was made by some of the philosophes of the eighteenth-century Enlightenment who endeavored to substitute a "religion of humanity" for that of Christianity. During the nineteenth century, and particularly in Victorian England, the influence of the Darwinian evolutionary hypothesis led to a major renewal of the effort to create a true "humanism" by reformulating ethics on a non-theistic basis and in the light of Darwin's ideas. To this end a number of literary figures and academic philosophers undertook the construction of a philosophy of humanism. Whether they succeeded or not is still a matter for some debate. Nevertheless, the movement has had a continuing and important effect. The significance of this modern humanism in its Victorian beginnings is discussed in the following essay.

Atheism has an ancestry far beyond the nineteenth century, and it would have been more wonderful if it had ceased to exist in Victorian times than if it had increased in its influence. The nineteenth century had itself been preceded by the Enlightenment, the "age of reason" when all men of sense held "reason" to be the right basis of human conduct and belief. But in Victorian times a significant change took place, one which is still in process of working itself out: the belief in reason had formerly been of a philosophical nature, but it became firmly rooted in the method and application of science. This was a new phase in the history of thought.

Once such a change had taken place in the foundations of non-religious thought, further changes took place in the line of thought involved. Through the Victorian age there was a change from the

* Reprinted with the permission of the author, the editors of the *Hibbert Journal* (LIX, 1962, 133–140), and George Allen & Unwin, Ltd., Publishers, with omission.

kind of rationalism which one associates with the Enlightenment to
that to be associated with the name of T. H. Huxley; and there was a
further change from the latter's agnosticism to a broader and deeper
humanism represented in the intellectual families, intricately inter-
connected, of the upper middle-class.

Different terms can be used, and indeed ought to be used, to describe
the different phases of *un*faith. Rationalism lays emphasis on the
supremacy of reason; this is still found in the memorandum of the
Rationalist Press Association:

Rationalism is the mental attitude which unreservedly accepts the
supremacy of reason and aims at establishing a system of philosophy and
ethics verifiable by experience and independent of all arbitrary assumptions
or authority.

That statement comes straight out of the nineteenth century, and is
not of course the worse for that; but it is, deliberately, narrow.
Huxley's coinage, agnosticism, covers a wider outlook; as he wrote:

When I reached intellectual maturity and began to ask myself whether
I was an Atheist, a Theist or a Pantheist; a Materialist or an Idealist; a
Christian or a Freethinker; I found that the more I learned and reflected,
the less ready was the answer, until, at last, I came to the conclusion that
I had neither art nor part with any of these denominations, except the last.
The one thing which most of these good people were agreed upon was
the one thing in which I differed from them. They were quite sure that
they had attained a certain "gnosis"—had, more or less successfully, solved
the problem of existence; while I was sure I had not, and had a pretty
strong conviction that the problem was insoluble. So I took thought, and
invented what I conceived to be the appropriate title of "Agnostic". It
came into my head as suggestively antithetic to the "Gnostic" of Church
history, who professed to know so much about the very things of which
I was ignorant.   (*Science and Christian Tradition*).

Thus, agnosticism is wider than rationalism, for it acknowledges the
existence of the unknowable; but it is none the less based on reason.

Secularism is another term, but it comes into this discussion less
markedly, simply because it is more a matter of practical politics than
of thought; it is the application, for instance in education, of rationalist
or agnostic principles. But it has some importance as a general term
to cover the various strands of unbelief of early Victorian times, since
it covers not only the thought of the intellectual classes but the
practical struggle for social betterment of the working classes. Finally,

there is humanism, a term which widened and deepened in its meaning towards the end of the century, taking into itself the earlier thought of rationalism and agnosticism. Humanism is of course a word of many meanings, but in its modern meaning it is rooted in the latter part of the nineteenth century. The promotion of human interests, as a proper end of life, interpreting "interests" in no narrow and exclusive sense but to include all the products of human culture and civilization, became a rational attitude of mind. This does not mean that reason was superseded, but that it was reinforced by other aspects of human experience. Whether or not one accepts humanism as an adequate philosophy, it is still worth respect as a fine result of the Victorian era.

It is no longer easy to imagine how violent were the polemics of religious controversy in Victorian times. From time to time we are reminded that the elements of the worst kind of controversy still exist. But they stand out by their very rarity; a century ago they were commonplace. This was not entirely the fault of the clerics; the violent anti-religion of the early part of the century was expressed in no mild terms, at any rate by the followers of Thomas Paine. The gradual reception of a rational, and ultimately humanist, attitude came from the appreciation by the educated classes of the significance of scientific advance, and of biblical scholarship.

The development of biblical criticism, centred at first and for many years in Germany, showed that it was no longer possible to take the Bible as a literal record of revelation. Previous criticism of Christianity was not generally founded on biblical criticism. Such a man as Thomas Paine, for example, simply applied his common-sense in reading the Bible, and damaging though his criticism was it was not founded on biblical scholarship. Indeed, the theologians themselves did much to destroy the literal interpretation of the Bible. The importance of Strauss's *Life of Jesus* for English thought was fortuitously heightened by the fact that George Eliot translated it into English; but such publications as the *Essays and Reviews,* giving the broad church view in 1860, and *Lux Mundi,* giving the catholic view in 1889, continued the work, without intention, of creating and sustaining a humanist outlook. Perhaps the most paradoxical incident of all was that the *Encyclopaedia Biblica,* written by clerical and kindred authorities, was re-issued in the twentieth century by the Rationalist Press Association. The churches were themselves absorbing much of the rationalist criticism which was partly made by their own members, except for the Roman Catholic Church, which came to the dividing of the waters with the expulsion of such modernists as Loisy, and the proclamation of Papal Infallibility in 1870.

It is one of the numerous contradictions of the Victorian age that it was at once religious and irreligious. The reason was given by John Stuart Mill:

> It was natural that a philosophy which anathematized all that had been going on in Europe from Constantine to Luther, or even to Voltaire, should be succeeded by another, at once a severe critic of the new tendencies of society, and an impassioned vindicator of what was good in the past.   (*Mill on Bentham and Coleridge,* ed. F. R. Leavis).

In religious matters, evangelicalism exerted an influence in every class of society, although, as is now agreed, that influence was more superficial than it was then admitted to be. It set the tone, however, for the whole of society, so that speech and overt conduct changed in a couple of generations to an almost incredible degree. This was a largely superficial change, for the Victorian under-world, as Humphry House has put it, "reeked of sex." Nevertheless, lip-service was paid to the new virtue; by the early sixties. Thackeray was writing:

> I can see old gentlemen now among us, of perfect breeding, of quiet lives, with venerable grey heads, fondling their grandchildren; and look at them, and wonder what they were once. That gentleman of the grand old school, when he was in the 10th Hussars, and dined at the prince's table, would fall under it night after night . . . If, in the petulance of play or drink, that gentleman spoke a sharp word to his neighbour, he and the other would infallibly go out and try to shoot each other the next morning . . . That gentleman, so exquisitely polite with ladies in a drawing-room, so loftily courteous, if he talked now as he used among men in his youth, would swear so as to make your hair stand on end.   (*The Four Georges*).

And so on. The change was one of the fruits of evangelicalism. Against evangelicalism, the Tractarian movement helped to revive the Church of England. It was itself only a minority movement little heeded or known to the majority of the population, but in later days it had a profound effect on the lives of working people, if only by the schools, hospitals and charities centred on parish churches, not to mention the revival of religious orders whose members had a practical effect on the lives of the people.

Certainly it was an age of religion, and in many ways genuine religion, despite the mere respectability which made many people go to church regularly. Yet simultaneously there was growing up a more profound unbelief than ever had existed before. In fact, the difference from the previous century was not so much that those Victorians who thought about religion (and all who thought at all did think about it) were more or less religious than their ancestors, but that they took it seriously. New materials lay to hand, and had to be accounted for in religious discussion. Up to the nineteenth century, discussion of religion had been continued on the same basis for hundreds, if not thousands, of years. A Roman sceptic would have been as much at home discussing the validity or otherwise of Christianity with eighteenth-century sceptics as with his contomporaries. No more materials, essentially, lay to hand. With the nineteenth century not only did biblical criticism destroy the possibility of a literal interpretation of the scriptures, but natural science brought in new and, in their effects, devastating problems. Of these, the theory of evolution was the greatest.

True, the development of physics in previous centuries had already necessitated new views of the universe. As pictured by Newton, the universe was an unchanging one, affording a fit parallel with Paley's watch. The Newtonian universe did not evolve; it was in movement, but only as a machine moves—it simply kept going, once having been started at some unknown date in the past. The infiltration of evolutionary ideas completely altered the picture. This was by no means solely the work of Darwin. A dozen years before Darwin's *Origin of Species,* Chambers had published *Vestiges of Creation,* expounding an evolutionary theory of the development of life. This view was taking the place of the catastrophic theory already advanced to account for the multitude of fossils of extinct animals which were being discovered. Even the great Cuvier had been satisfied with catastrophism as an explanation, and it was still possible to reconcile that theory with the unchanging Newtonian universe.

The theory of evolution was dropped by Darwin into a soil already favourable for its reception owing to the tentative discussions which had been proceeding for many years. The challenge to Christianity had at last to be taken seriously. This challenge was taken up by heated protagonists, with such outstanding and dramatic incidents as the debate between Huxley and Wilberforce in the Sheldonian. Yet it was not only a matter of debate between science and religion: Wilberforce had been secretly coached by the great palæontologist, Richard Owen (a fact not revealed in the "official" life!), while Frederick Temple received the theory of evolution in the most friendly and reasonable manner. But the general outline of the debate is clear enough. It was only a matter of time before the theory had to be accepted, and reconciled with religion as best it could.

The important factor for the development of the line of thought here being considered was that the theory of evolution destroyed the belief in the special creation of man at a particular moment of history, and it destroyed the unique place of man in nature. It was evident that the world and man himself had existed for aeons, which was not, perhaps, so serious once the account given in the Book of Genesis was not taken literally any more. More serious was the placing of man in the evolutionary process, so that he no longer appeared unique; and more serious still was the demonstration that the evolutionary process was lacking in the moral elements hitherto regarded as basic to man's nature. Actually, the conclusions drawn need not have been so devastating; man is indeed unique, as modern biology has shown, though not in the old sense; and the evolutionary process has been shown to depend at least as much on co-operation as on competition, neither of which in nature can be compared with their human counterparts. But this lay many years in the future.

Faced with new discoveries of science, what was man to do? He must first face the agonies of rethinking his religious outlook. That a great deal of suffering was entailed by this process of breaking free from old and narrow bonds into a chilly world of freedom is undoubted. The literature of Victorian times abounds in the evidence: the dismay of Tennyson, the defiance of Browning, the melancholy of Arnold, the hysteria of Swinburne, the despair of Hardy, the stoicism of George Eliot—all these are evidence enough. Life was "one moment in annihilation's waste," as Fitzgerald put it. Whatever the reaction, a man had to choose a new way for himself.

It was impossible to abandon the scientific attitude, with its habitual analysis of the evidence. Nevertheless, the more percipient Victorians saw that analysis had its limitations. As John Stuart Mill had found, unrelenting analysis had evil effects:

I now saw, or thought I saw, what I had always before received with incredulity—that the habit of analysis has a tendency to wear away the feelings: as indeed it has, when no other mental habit is cultivated, and the analysing spirit remains without its natural complements and correctives . . . Analytic habits may thus even strengthen the associations between causes and effects, means and ends, but tend altogether to weaken those which are, to speak familiarly, a *mere* matter of feeling. They are therefore (I thought) favourable to prudence and clear-sightedness, but a perpetual worm at the root both of the passions and the virtues; and, above all, fearfully undermine all desires, and all pleasures, which are the effects of association, that is, according to the theory I held, all except the purely physical and organic; of the entire insufficiency of which to make life desirable, no one had a stronger conviction than I had. (*Autobiography*).

This was the danger which the agnostic faced, and it was the need to extend the range of human experience that led to a broader, but not shallower, attitude than rigid rationalism. Fortunately, to strengthen them in this new and chilly world, the Victorians had the inherited strength of Puritanism. Of this, Leslie Stephen wrote:

The old Puritan leaven is working yet in various forms, in spite of the ridicule of artistic minds and the contempt of philosophers.

And in such an outstanding example of great Victorian integrity as George Eliot, the Puritanic attitude provided strength in the greatest adversity, as Lord David Cecil observes:

The moral code founded on that Puritan theology had soaked itself too deeply into the fibre of her thought and feeling for her to give it up as well. She might not believe in heaven and hell and miracles, but she believed in right and wrong, and man's paramount obligation to follow right, as strictly as if she were Bunyan himself. And her standards of right and wrong were the Puritan standards. She admired truthfulness and chastity and industry and self-restraint, she disapproved of loose living and recklessness and deceit and self-indulgence. (*Early Victorian Novelists*).

Of course, the attitudes there summed up are not necessarily Puritanical (they are simply the attitudes of decent people in all ages), but they were strengthened by the survival of a tradition. Evangelicalism had done much to provide that strength (so, in another way, had the Oxford Movement), and the zeal of religious reform was in large part transferred to the advocacy of agnosticism. And as the century advanced, the necessary connection between secularism and "progressive" politics became less clear. It was indeed the older rationalists who remained radicals. It was characteristic that Charles Bradlaugh's journal *The National Reformer* should be subtitled "Radical Advocate and Free-thought Journal," and in its last issue be described as having been consistently "Republican, Atheistic, and Malthusian." Similarly, G. J. Holyoake's autobiography was aptly entitled *Sixty Years of an Agitator's Life,* for he was both a founder of the Co-operative Movement and a leader of secularism. For many years practical advocacy of rationalism owed much to its association with radical politics, but when the trend towards socialism became more specific later in the century, the association wore thin.

As rationalism was being absorbed into a broader agnosticism, so the latter began to be absorbed in an even broader humanism. The "religion of humanity," in a formal sense, was never more than the fad of a comparative few, but it was the precursor of the new humanism. Beatrice Webb has described the situation in her youth:

> In the particular social and intellectual environment in which I lived, this stream of tendencies culminated in Auguste Comte's union of the "religion of humanity" with a glorification of science, in opposition to both theology and metaphysics, as the final stage in the development of the human intellect.   (*My Apprenticeship*).

In such an environment, the extreme narrowness of the old rationalism, and the somewhat terrified rectitude of the old agnosticism, were replaced by a broad humane culture. Beatrice Webb indicates the cultural milieu in which she lived:

> And whether we girls took down from the well-filled library shelves the *Confessions of St. Augustine* or those of Jean Jacques Rousseau, whether the parcel from Hatchett's contained the latest novels by Guy de Maupassant and Emile Zola or the learned tomes of Auguste Comte or Ernest Renan; whether we ordered from the London Library or from Mudie's a pile of books on Eastern religions, or a heterogeneous selection of what I will call "yellow" literature, was determined by our own choice or by the suggestion of any casual friend or acquaintance. When we complained to my father that a book we wanted to read was banned by the libraries: "Buy it, my dear," was his automatic answer.   (*My Apprenticeship*).

In such circumstances, among such families as Beatrice Webb describes, the broadening into humanism was, perhaps not inevitable, but certainly frequent. As this happened, the revolutionary discoveries of science were accepted into their proper place in the complex of human activities and interests. This humanist attitude was not rooted in a religion or a philosophy, but in a recognition of the position of humanity on the earth. One of the most brilliant of the earlier rationalists, W. K. Clifford, before his too-early death in 1879, had written:

> . . . to do as well as possible what we can do best; to work for the improvement of the social organisation; to seek earnestly after truth and only to accept provisionally opinions one has not enquired into; to regard men as comrades in work and their freedom as a sacred thing; in fact, to recognise the enormous and fearful difference between truth and falsehood, right

and wrong, and how truth and right are to be got by free enquiry and the love of our comrades for their own sake and nobody else.

(The Ethics of Belief).

Such was, and is, the humanist's creed. Of humanism, G. D. Klingopulos has recently said:

Gradually in the course of the Victorian era, and almost unconsciously, there developed amongst the increasingly large number of literate men and women a humanist attitude to life which was not a matter of creeds and dogmas or their denial, but of recognition and acceptance of the human condition, or loves, loyalties, duties, respect for intelligence and feelings, which are not less relevant to religion than to art and science . . . Though it offers no transcendence except in unattended moments and no answers to ultimate questions, humanism helps to keep alive a sense of their importance and to maintain standards of sincerity, delicacy, and intellectual honesty by which religion itself must be judged.

(From Dickens to Hardy, ed. Boris Ford).

That is a fair, if critical, summary. What may be added is that even the Victorian phase of humanism must be seen as part of a long humanist tradition. As was observed at the beginning, atheism is of ancient origin; but the development of Victorian humanism, incorporating both old and new aspects of secularism, enables us to see that there is also a humanist tradition of which the Victorian phase is only an important part. What late Victorian humanism did was to lay the foundations for modern humanism, and to alter the humanist tradition. By now, Victorian humanism can be seen to be not only a broadening out from, and away from eighteenth-century rationalism; it is also the foundation of twentieth-century humanism. Whether twentieth-century humanism is "a faith to live by," to use a cant expression of the day, is not here the question; but what is certain is that the transition in Victorian times disposed for ever of *mere* rationalism, and of *mere* agnosticism; but not of *mere* humanism. And for that, whether we are religious or not, we owe a debt of gratitude to those great Victorian humanist families—the Arnolds, the Huxleys, the Stephens, the Macaulays, the Trevelyans, and the like—who made a culture out of a dogmatic quarrel.

BIBLIOGRAPHY

Noel Annan, *Leslie Stephen. His Thought and Character in Relation to His Time* (Cambridge, Mass.: 1952), particularly chaps. IV–VIII. Elliott-Binns, *Religion in the Victorian Era.* Thomas McPherson, "Henry Sidgwick and the *Methods of Ethics,*" *Church Quarterly Review,* CLVII

(1956), 453–462. Frank Manuel, *The Prophets of Paris* [Turgot, Condorcet, Saint-Simon, Fourier, and Comte] (Cambridge, Mass.: 1962). Howard Murphy, "The Ethical Revolt against Christian Orthodoxy in Early Victorian England," *American Historical Review,* LX (1955), 800–817. Basil Willey, *Nineteenth Century Studies* (London: 1949); *More Nineteenth Century Studies: a Group of Honest Doubters* (London: 1956). [The Editor.]

THE CHANGING IMPACT OF DARWIN ON PHILOSOPHY *

John Herman Randall, Jr.

If the shock of Darwinism seemed for a time to unhinge the bulwarks of Victorian religious faith, the result in the long run for certain systems of thought and belief was less disastrous than it appeared to be. Some forms of idealistic philosophy and Christian theology, particularly in Continental Europe, were able to incorporate the Darwinian hypothesis with relative ease because the way had been prepared by generations of philosophers and speculative theologians whose thought already tended in that direction. Men, as Professor Randall indicates, were not prepared at once to give up the idea of God's existence, and they sought, where possible, to harmonize traditional beliefs with the new doctrines. The result was a continuous reworking of points of view in the hope of comprehending and synthesizing this very influential scientific idea. As a consequence, some schools of philosophy and theology found an intellectual stimulus in Darwinism. The process of comprehension and stimulation is described in the selection that follows.

Darwin's ideas came into an intellectual world admirably prepared to welcome them. The great problem of cultural assimilation in the XIXth century was the religious problem. The century started with all human interests and values more deeply bound up, in philosophical idealism and the various currents of Romanticism, with a theistic world-

---

* Reprinted with the permission of the author and the editors of the *Journal of the History of Ideas* (XXII, 1961, 435–462, with omissions).

view than at any time since the XIIIth century. And then, with the steady advance of science, men came to feel that such a religious philosophy was untenable: "science" just could not be disregarded. The XIXth century started with a Romantic faith in an anthropocentric universe; science went on with steady assurance to undermine that faith.

Today, when the problem generating philosophical answers is not cosmic, but social, and focuses on adjustment, not to new knowledge of the universe—the religious problem—but on what is to us obviously a far greater problem, to the forces of industrial society, including its apparent capacity for committing suicide, it is the social philosophies of the XIXth century that have come to our perspectives to seem the most important. We find it today hard to understand how the cosmic religious problem could ever have seemed to men central. So we are tempted to make the crucial impact of Darwin on men's thinking what we have come to call "social Darwinism," with Richard Hofstadter. But I myself, with my father before me, lived through it all. And I can assure the younger reader that social Darwinism had no emotional impact on men's lives: the very term had not been invented. But the religious problem was profoundly disruptive.

With such a central cultural experience, the men of the XIXth century were looking desperately for a new religious faith, a new Cosmic Companion, an up-to-date "scientific" God. How intensely they pursued this quest is abundantly clear from the letters of the great Victorians. Men so much wanted to believe in God and Providence, that they grasped at any straw. God was Spencer's "the Unknowable" (which he got from Dean Mansel), God was "energy," God was the "principle of concretion"—somewhere, in some scientific or pseudo-scientific concept, lurked the Father of mankind, still exercising his divine providence. Men wanted to believe in God, because they simply could not order their lives without him. William James in his early crisis well illustrates this demand for a cosmic sanction for the good life. The idealists had staked everything on God: he must exist in—or behind—the scientific universe.

This "scientific universe" came from the detailed working-out of mechanistic explanation. But this idea seemed to the traditionalists less violent a shock than the new idea of man's animal origins, for it had been in the world since the time of Descartes and the XVIIth century. But to the educated, it seemed far more inexorable. Science was rapidly making advances, filling in the details of the Cartesian and Newtonian program. The results were so impressive, that by the

1850's they could no longer be disregarded. This "alien world" seemed intolerable to the men of the mid-century, in its complete disregard of man's interests and values. We must not forget that "nature red in tooth and claw" was written nine years before the *Origin of Species*. *In Memoriam* appeared in 1850, and Tennyson was nothing if not a "representative" figure.

In the mid-XIXth century, this "scientific universe" took the form of sweeping generalizations: the law of the conservation of energy, the laws of thermo-dynamics, the mechanistic theory of life, above all, an unyielding mechanistic determinism. The laboratory had not yet unearthed so many facts that no generalization could embrace them all. The recent breakdown of the Newtonian philosophy of nature—as distinct from Newton's "natural philosophy," or science—had not yet occurred. The idea that all such general formulations are "leading principles" of scientific investigation, instruments to guide inquiry, rather than "laws of governing" the universe, received as yet little support, though such views were being made central by Charles S. Peirce in the 1860's, as one of the first real implications of Darwin's thought.

The most speculative generalizations of the scientists, either abandoned or greatly modified today, were seized on to complete the picture of the "scientific world." XIXth-century science, though impressively richer than Newtonian mechanics, clung to the same fundamental assumption of a closed mechanical and material order. It was in fact far closer to the crude and simple systems of the XVIIth century than to the tentative, cautious, experimental science of today, with its world of radiant energy. With this Newtonian framework, not yet burst asunder, with these dogmatic assumptions, men felt they had to come to terms.

The popularization and speedy establishment of Darwinian evolution came at the psychological moment. Evolution was a genuine Godsend to the religious seekers after escape from the alien world. Here, in the very heart of "science" itself, was obviously the new faith needed and so greatly yearned after. There is a purpose in the world, man's ideals do matter to nature, heaven will be reached, in substantial form, on earth. As Edward Rowland Sills put it, "Some call it evolution, / Others call it God."

Evolution was eagerly accepted as a substitute religious faith. It was taken as a great help—if not even the complete answer—to the religious problem of harmonizing faith with reason and science. Just so, the earlier adjuster and mediator, Thomas Aquinas, had eagerly seized on Aristotelian science as the great instrument for harmoniz-

ing faith with "reason" in the XIIIth century. This, incidentally, is
why Leo XIII, in his encyclical *Aeterni Patris* in 1879, turned to
Thomas Aquinas to solve for the Catholic Church the XIXth-century
religious problem.

The cosmic evolutionary philosophies of the XIXth-century adjusters
were so busy trying to find a new cosmic faith, a new and up-to-
date God and Providence, in "the" evolutionary process, that they
quite failed to realize what evolution really implied. And the important part of Darwin's theory for the more recent fourth group, the
transformers, was quite overlooked: the biological character and settling
of human experience. In fact, the idea of "evolution" remained
throughout the XIXth century basically a Romantic conception. In
its origin, it started with the Romanticists, with Goethe, Herder,
Schelling, and Hegel. It was forced on biology after it had been long
dominant in history and the social sciences and theology. It was accepted by the cosmic evolutionary philosophers, not as a mere scientific biological theory, but as a principle of cosmic explanation, as a
new primary cause, the true form of God's will and providence—that
is, as a new Romantic faith, the greatest and most seductive of the
great Romantic faiths.

This is obvious in a man like Bergson. But it is just as true of
Herbert Spencer. For him, evolution is as much a religious faith as for
Hegel or Marx. And his famous "law of evolution"·

Evolution is an integration of matter and a concomitant dissipation of
motion, during which the matter passes from an indefinite, incoherent
homogeneity to a definite, coherent heterogeneity, and during which the
retained motion undergoes a parallel transformation

is as much an idealistic attempt to construct the world ápriori as
anything in Hegel. And it is less justified: for Hegel's formula does
apply to some kinds of cultural change.

I have said, Darwin's ideas came into an intellectual world admirably prepared to receive them. Not only did they come as the
answer to the central cultural problem of the time, the religious problem; for about a century, evolutionary ideas had been enjoying a
growing popularity. In biology itself, after the XVIIIth-century ex-
plorations of such ideas by Buffon, Robinet, Diderot, and Lamarck,
they had been losing ground. The opposition of Cuvier, and the lack
of a plausible explanation of the method of evolution, before Darwin's
natural selection, seemed to create an impasse.

But in most other fields, evolution was becoming an increasingly popular idea. It took two major forms, which actually constituted the faiths the adjusters took Darwin as supporting from biology. On the one hand was the notion of a liberal, "rationalistic" evolution, bound up with the idea of "progress" in human history. On the other was the cosmic evolution of Romantic idealism. This form, starting with the evolution of man's religion, in Lessing and Herder, culminated in the full temporalizing of the great chain of being in Schelling—still in a religious interest.

The first form was French and British. Its classic statement is in Condorcet's *Progress of the Human Mind* (1794), written in prison in the shadow of the guillotine, yet expressing a magnificent faith. Condorcet summed up a half-century of French analysis of man's perfectibility. Condorcet's English disciple was William Godwin, who, ironically, provoked Malthus who was to suggest to Darwin natural selection as the mechanism of evolution, and thus reinstate Godwin's own views. This is also the background of Spencer's pre-Darwinian "Progress: Its Law and Cause"; as well as of Saint-Simon, also inspired in prison, and through him, of Comte's Law of the Three Stages.

The second form was primarily German. It began in religion, in Lessing's *Education of the Human Race* (1780); in Herder's *Philosophy of History* (1774) and *Ideas for the History of Man* (1784). It was made cosmic in Schelling's evolutionary metaphysics: his *Philosophy of Nature* displays nature as the evolutionary manifestation of the Absolute. Oken develops the same general conception. Hegel did not temporalize his philosophy of nature: there is no biological evolution of species in Hegel, as in Schelling. But Hegel has a chain of being, a series of levels, easily temporalized by later Hegelians after Darwin. And, as the great idealist of social experience, Hegel made fundamental the evolution of human society, institutions and culture—everything he called *Geist*. In fact, the later cosmic evolutionary philosophers were overwhelmingly Hegelian in character, with a change only in the new biological terminology adopted. Alexander Humboldt in his *Kosmos* (1845–58) offered an impressive evolutionary system of scientific knowledge. With these men must be grouped those who pursued the Hegelian idea of social evolution, the left-wing Hegelians of the '40's, including Feuerbach and Marx.

These varieties of evolutionary ideas in philosophy, as distinguished from biological theory, which has its own story, were prevalent for a century before 1859. This fact explains why Darwin had so immediate a welcome from scholars in history, the social sciences, and philosophy. It also explains why they pretty uniformly misunderstood him, why they took him as merely reinforcing their own ideas, long familiar, and why they failed to see the real significance of his ideas. In the last analysis, it explains why they were adjusters, harmonizers of old and new, and not transformers. These were the cosmic evolutionary faiths Darwin was first taken as substantiating.

How biological evolution would be speedily brought to the support of faiths already worked out in the pre-Darwinian era, especially of the faiths of Romantic idealism, was, however, not immediately recognized in 1859. This was especially the case in England and America, where religious orthodoxy, the heritage of the great religious revivals of the first half of the century, was still strongly entrenched.

Its hold had been broken in Germany, where religion was now dominated by the great idealistic and humanistic reinterpretations of the nature and function of religion that were the German heritage from Romantic idealism. These included the three main forms of XIXth-century "liberal" religion, of the theology of divine immanence. The first was the Hegelian interpretation, making religion a form of philosophical knowledge, expressed in religious symbols. The second was the Ritschlian, making it a form of moral action, of ethical idealism. The third was that of Schleiermacher, making it a form of religious feeling and experience. To these three German religious currents, Darwinian or biological evolution was quite congenial. It reinforced their own philosophy of monism, and of the immanence of the divine. They had all been long accustomed to viewing God as the force behind cosmic evolution, and to finding purpose and values in nature. Thus later American representatives of these German theologies, the modernists and "liberal" theologians of the end of the century, became in the U.S.A. the strongest champions of Darwin, men like Lyman Abbott, Henry Churchill King, and other Schleiermacherians and Ritschlians. But to these German religious currents, Darwin seemed also rather irrelevant: he offered little of novelty in the way of the ideas that interested them.

In France, Darwin did not appear too disruptive either. There anti-clerical and secular thought was strong. It took two main forms. There was first the evolutionary "spiritualism" of Victor Cousin, based largely on Schelling. Cousin's school produced imposing works on historical evolution. Secondly, there was the cultural evolutionism of the Positivists. Both welcomed and interpreted Darwin. The former developed a strong school of idealistic evolutionists, culminating in the next generation in Bergson's creative evolution.

In England and America, there had been little reinterpretation of religion before 1859; that had to wait for the next generation. The only exception had been Coleridge and the still small party of Broad Churchmen; and the American Transcendentalists, among the tiny minority of New England Unitarianism. So in America there was no large religious party to welcome Darwin; the full shock of the naturalization of man was felt there. Darwin was taken as completing the picture of the "scientific universe"; he became the symbol of the scientific faith, for two generations, till he was superseded by Einstein. Accept evolution, and you had abandoned mere tradition. Darwin was the gateway to emancipation, to freedom from a literal orthodoxy. Such liberation brought the freedom to embrace one of two alternatives; the religion of science, in one of the XIXth-century mechanistic versions, or an idealistic reinterpretation of both religion and science. The first alternative had great popular appeal. The second made by far the wider appeal to those with religious and humanistic interests, to the academic class, who teach and support American philosophy.

In other words, the impact of Darwin was to foster simultaneously the popular philosophies of evolutionary materialism, and the academic philosophies of idealistic reinterpretation and reconstruction. Thus in England and America it was Darwinian evolution that provoked the idealistic protest against the scientific universe and the alien world, and the idealistic reconstructions of the religious tradition; philosophic idealism was dominant in academic circles till about 1900. In Germany, the idealistic protest and reconstruction had been accomplished in the first half of the century, long before Darwin. Idealism possessed its own version of evolution, in Hegelian or Schellingian forms. Hence it found Darwin either irrelevant, or else a mere additional support. In France, Darwin either strengthened the existing Positivistic evolutionism, or else supported the secular ethical idealism in its opposition to mechanistic Positivism, on what was the central philosophical problem in France from 1870 to 1914, the issue of determinism *vs.* freedom. French ethical idealism worked out a philosophy of "creative evolution" in which evolution was made to tip the scales for freedom.

BIBLIOGRAPHY

Philip Appleman *et al.* (eds.), *1859: Entering an Age of Crisis* (Bloomington, Ind.: 1959). Loren C. Eiseley, *Darwin's Century* (Garden City, N.Y.: 1958). Donald Fleming, "The Century of the *Origin of Species*," *Journal of the History of Ideas*, XX (1959), 437–446. Charles C. Gillispie, *Genesis and Geology* (New York: 1959). John C. Greene, *Darwin and the Modern World View* (Baton Rouge, La.: 1961). Gertrude Himmelfarb, *Darwin and the Darwinian Revolution* (Garden City, N.Y.: 1959). Sol Tax and Charles Callander (eds.), *Evolution after Darwin*, Vol. III: *Issues in Evolution* (Chicago: 1960). Basil Willey, *Darwin and Butler: Two Versions of Evolution* (New York: 1960). [The Editor.]

THE CATHOLIC CHURCH AND SCIENCE *

P. E. Hodgson

As we have seen, one of the great conflicts within the context of western religious history has involved the claims of scientific truth against the truths of revealed religion. In the last two or three centuries this conflict has sometimes resulted in a deadlock between various religious denominations and scientific thinkers attempting to put forward an unfamiliar hypothesis that seemed to invalidate long accepted Christian teachings. Among scientists, as a result, there has often been a tendency to regard Christianity as a repressive check upon scientific development. Here we may not overlook the fact that on more than one famous occasion—most notably in the cases of Galileo and Darwin— serious efforts were made by some religious groups to halt the spread of ideas that seemed inimical to the teachings of Scripture or to beliefs that, over the centuries, had come to be accepted as true in the Christian sense. On the other hand, we must not forget the equally important fact that for most Christians the phenomena of the natural world were always acceptable insofar as they could be understood to be part of God's creation. Whatever is is the result of God's will and therefore cannot conflict with His revelation. It is in the latter sense that the author of the following selection, a scientist and a Roman Catholic Christian, undertakes to show what the attitude of his own church is toward the findings of science. Although the Roman Catholic view of these matters differs from that of some other denominations, in a broad way, it is also shared by a great many persons of all faiths.

---

* Reprinted with the permission of the author, the editors of the *Hibbert Journal* (LIV, 1955–56, 15–28, with omissions), and George Allen & Unwin, Ltd., Publishers.

The first stage in scientific investigation is the collection of many facts about the phenomenon being studied. If possible, measurements are made as well. These facts are classified and compared, and particular note taken of any correlations that exist between the different types of observations or measurements. This stage is often called, for obvious reasons, the natural history stage.

But the scientist is not satisfied with a collection of facts; he wants to unify them and if possible gain some insight into the inter-relations between them and the mechanisms underlying them. This is done by theories. A close study of the facts, helped by a deeper knowledge of similar phenomena, may suggest such a theory to him. From this theory he can deduce what would be observed if the theory were true, and these predictions may be compared with the results of experiment. If the theory disagrees with the experimentally observed facts it must be modified or discarded; if it agrees with them the scientist goes on to predict new phenomena with it, and test it again and so on. The theory will often suggest new experiments, and will show what measurements should be made and which may be ignored. Science normally advances in this way by a complex interaction between theory and experiment; the "natural history" stage is appropriate only to branches of science whose fundamentals are still obscure.

The important point to notice for our purpose is that a scientific theory is not deduced logically from the facts of experiment; it is a creation of the human mind whose consequences agree, so far as we know, with experience. It often happens that a new fact is discovered which necessitates the modification or abandonment of a well-supported theory. The facts remain always the same, but theories are often transient and one follows another in the advance of science.

As the scientist continues with his investigations he may find that his theory gives him a very detailed knowledge of the phenomena and enables him to predict their course with confidence in circumstances far removed from those in which he has studied it. Then it may be said that his knowledge has passed beyond the merely hypothetical, and that he has attained a real insight into the phenomena concerned. Thus what begins as a tentative hypothesis may finally be accepted as true. An example of a theory that is practically certain is the atomic theory of matter and, although I am not a biologist, it seems that the theory of evolution in its general form can be placed in the same category. The certainty we can attain concerning these theories is of course only a moral certainty, and not a metaphysical, theological or mathematical certainty.

A closer analysis shows that this distinction between facts and theories is by no means so sharp or so simple as might appear at first sight. We are not simply passive receptors of sense-impressions, we interpret and select them in a way that depends on our previous experiences, so that what we consider as facts depends to some extent on our theories. Nevertheless it is a useful distinction provided that its limitations are kept in mind.

Now that the nature of science has been considered, albeit in a very sketchy fashion, it is possible to investigate its relationship with various systems of religious belief, particularly Christianity. Before examining the place of science in Christian thought, it is of interest to see how science flourishes in the intellectual climates of different religions, for this furnishes a good indication of the esteem in which science is held by them. The important point is the attitude to the material world inherent in them. Thus if a religion teaches that the world is an illusion and that the way to spiritual perfection lies in increasing emancipation from it, science is hardly likely to flourish. Perhaps this is at least part of the reason why science as we know it did not develop in the great civilisations of the East. Worse still, some religions, for example Manicheeism and Albigensianism, have taught that matter is inherently evil, and one who believes this is even less likely to become a scientist than one who believes it to be an illusion.

What then is the Christian view of matter? The Church teaches that this world was created by God for man to live in. Matter is therefore inherently and essentially good, and it is not only legitimate but praiseworthy for man to study it by the methods of science, for in doing so he is fulfilling God's purpose. The Church therefore encourages scientific investigation, confident that no fact that could ever be discovered about God's world could conflict with the revealed truth entrusted to its care.

Although scientific knowledge is good, it does not follow that it is legitimate to use any means to obtain it. For example, the German doctors were not justified in using concentration-camp victims for their medical experiments. Every scientist is primarily a man and only secondarily a scientist, and so it is not good for him to spend all his time on scientific research. He must take care to acquire a broad knowledge so that he can appreciate the limitations of science and its part in the whole of knowledge. Lastly, he must be ever mindful of the effects that his discoveries may have on human society, and it is his duty to do all he can to minimise the evil effects and enhance the good ones.

The Church has always insisted that matter is good and thus worthy of study. Throughout its history it has fought a relentless battle against the Manichees and all who hold that matter is inherently evil or even somewhat disreputable. In the Middle Ages this attitude was rampant in sects which held that sex and marriage are evil. In England it contributed to Puritanism, and elements of it survive to-day.

The Christian recognises two sources of Revelation, or ways that God speaks to man, the Natural and Supernatural. The first is the revelation contained in the created world and the second the revelation contained in the Scriptures and interpreted by the Church. He will therefore welcome every fact established by science as increasing his knowledge of God's world. As both natural and supernatural revelation come from God, they cannot come into conflict. If ever an apparent conflict arises the Christian knows that it is due to a lack of understanding either of the scientific result, or of the Christian doctrine, or of the relationship between the two, and will wait for its resolution in the light of further knowledge.

BIBLIOGRAPHY

F. L. Baumer, *Religion and the Rise of Scepticism,* chap. v. Bernhard Bavink, *Science and God* (New York: 1934). R. G. Collingwood, *The Idea of Nature* (Oxford: 1945). Herbert Dingle, "Science and Religion," *The Scientific Adventure* (London: 1952), 350–363. Karl Heim, *Christian Faith and Natural Science* (New York: 1953). Werner Heisenberg, *Physics and Philosophy* (New York: 1958). J. W. N. Sullivan, *The Contemporary Mind: Some Modern Answers* (London: 1934). Sol Tax and Charles Callander (eds.), *Evolution after Darwin,* Vol. III: *Issues in Evolution* (Chicago: 1960). [The Editor.]

JUDAISM AND THE AGE OF ANXIETY *

Arthur J. Zuckerman

In the summer days of 1914 the western world finished an era which, despite its imperfections and dissidence, sometimes seems in retrospect far more certain in its outlook and secure in its values than anything we have known since. The outbreak of the First World War is often regarded as the beginning of an era of neo-barbarism, an "age of anxiety," in which the historic process wherein western civilization sought to realize the best of its traditional ideals came to an abrupt end. Total war, mass annihilation, irrational philosophies, totalitarian government, and, more recently, the threat of nuclear destruction have evoked a continuous questioning not only among religious believers but among thoughtful people everywhere. In this atmosphere of alarm and doubt most religious groups have sought a reaffirmation of traditional beliefs. The following selection undertakes to describe Judaism's response to this time of troubles and to reaffirm the positive values of that ancient faith. Although there are historic divergences in point of view between Judaism and Christianity, both faiths have a confidence in the divine ordering of things, which has had a significant influence on the historic development of the West.

Our period has all but earned the epithet—the age of the failure of nerve. From the standpoint of scientific advance, it has been called the atomic age; and those who are best informed have emphasized that this connotes a fundamentally new era for mankind. From the standpoint of psychology and religion, our time has been dubbed the age of anxiety. Actually, these two appellations interpenetrate one another. The frightful power of atomic energy clutches at people's nerves and disorients them; while their state of anxiety paralyzes efforts towards its use for constructive purposes. He who works with young people, to whom the draft and war are a clinging miasma, knows the mental and moral and intellectual up-rootings that have loosed them from the shaky moorings which once weakly held them. It is no surprise that some of our young people act as if they were caught in an inextricable

---

* Reprinted with the permission of the editors of *The Reconstructionist* (XIX, No. 7, May 1953, 9–16, with omissions).

web of circumstances, wherein they entangle themselves only more deeply the more they struggle to strike free. A mood of indecision, deriving from a yearning for escape and the poignant realization that there is no escape, has gripped not a few of them. Apathy is apparent and an ill-concealed contempt for reason and the methods of the intellect. In such a state of mind, the "turn to religion" may smack of a drive for "opium" in a flight from responsibility to narcosis.

Nor do we lack the "narcotics peddlers" who openly hawk the theme of futility, horror and the meaninglessness of all that roots in man; the plaint of his incapacity to control or transcend the environment he himself has created.

There have arisen in our time poets and artists and prophets of despair, spokesmen of futility and negation, who reflect the mood of our time and deepen its penetration into men's souls. And although the college student of the 1960's may be a poor reader, the mass media of communication are so avid today for the materials of frustration, anguish and indecision, that they help to create a cultural climate which molds the minds and hearts of the young like putty.

Widely known and still read is Franz Kafka. Although he died [in 1924] the recent appearance of his works in English translation has made of Kafka a major spokesman of our age of anxiety. Kafka's novels, *The Trial* and *The Castle,* present his heroes—intentionally symbols of humanity—as victims of utterly cruel and capricious forces, inscrutable and implacable. *The Castle* is an allegory of man's yearning for divine grace and salvation. But man is altogether incapable of attaining such a goal by his own efforts. In fact, everyone of K's (the anonymous hero's) acts carries him farther and farther from his objective, symbolized by the Castle on the Hill. Here function the Heavenly Powers as a vast and almighty bureaucracy, frequently immoral, insatiably cruel, always inscrutable, blocking and frustrating K at every turn. The heartbreaking attempts of Kafka's hero to establish the right relationship with the Castle Powers constitute the drama of the novel and the stuff of the allegory. Still more disturbing is the village people's awe, even deep veneration, for these Powers that are so heartless and unresponsive to man's striving. Kafka, a descendant of the Hebrew prophets, can find no word of protest against this situation. For him, anguish and anxiety have become the inescapable condition of human existence.

Poets of frustration and negation are by no means new in cultural history. They are in fact very old. In far away antiquity they expressed the sense of alienation of early man buffeted by natural forces beyond his control—by wind and flood and earthquake, heat and drought and cold—all relentless and inscrutable. But where such poets and philosophers have been influential, they have undermined morale and shattered nerve and have marched in the vanguard of their culture on its way to disintegration and decay.

In ancient Babylonia, for example, there was current a story of the Flood, transformed later by the Hebrew genius and given the ethical orientation which now appears in the biblical version. But in the form of the Gilgamesh Epic it was as much a cry of frustration and negation of values as is Kafka's *Castle*. For what is the Epic's motivation for the Flood and the reduction of mankind thereby to sticky clay? Not men's immortality or depravity, which explains the Hebrew God's disappointment and His determination to start mankind off anew with the upright Noah. It is rather the cruelty and depravity of the gods, their internecine conflict and the caprice of the chief of them who hits upon the Flood as the means of terrifying and overwhelming his cosmic opponents. In the process, mankind is to be destroyed, but why should that restrain any god? In fact, when it turns out that *Utnapishtim* has escaped drowning, the chief deity flares with anger. In another ancient version of the Epic, the same god decrees destruction because mankind has become so numerous and noisy that they disturb him in his attempts at slumber! Clearly, we have in this Epic the projection of the ancient's sense of alienation from his gods, a picture of his cringing in a world where he could not really feel at home because it was ruled by arbitrary and cruel powers beyond his control. Like an anguished echo down the hall of time resound the words of the contemporary A. E. Housman, "I am a stranger and afraid in a world I never made."

The sense of alienation, of being victimized or, at least, sharply restricted by relentless and inscrutable forces, reappears in some Greek tragedies just before the decline of Athens and presages that "failure of nerve" to which has been traced the collapse of Hellenic culture. Of several ready examples, *Oedipus Rex* pursues to its bitter end the fate of Oedipus, who is destined to murder his father and marry his own mother, all unwittingly. Despite every effort to block the design of fate, it all happens exactly as pre-ordained, and there are even offspring of the strange union. Then the facts become known. In despair, the mother-wife commits suicide; in fearful anguish, her husband-son gouges out his eyes.

The twentieth century paganisms have deified the mighty authoritarian-totalitarian state—arbitrary, insatiably cruel and immoral, pseudo-scientific and militaristic. In this contemporary form, the ancient demons, fates and furies have usurped power again, and have once more terrified and alienated man from his fellow-man and the cosmos. But in the secular culture of the twentieth century, it is no longer possible to call them by supernatural names. They are seen to be what they always were in reality: the creatures of man himself, the projection of his own fears, frustrations and aggressions. So man is detected as the scoundrel he always was and the cause of his own predicament. And the unwarranted conclusion is now drawn that the seat of all evil is in that which is essentially human; man's mind, heart and will. Degeneracy is re-established as man's very nature. Humanness becomes the source of humanity's alienation: man is trapped by the carapace of his own evil, incapable of striking free by his own efforts.

God is just. So the Judge of all the earth must Himself do justly, as Abraham is made to remind God gently. Sodom and Gomorrah are threatened with destruction not because of God's willfulness and caprice but because of the evil and oppression therein. Strict justice condemns these cities, yet Abraham easily activates divine mercy so that fifty or forty or even ten righteous individuals would have sufficed to avert the evil decree.

Bulky segments of the Tradition, not just isolated words and phrases tucked away in crevices and hiding places, affirm the security which the Jew felt as the object of God's benevolence and assert his willingness to share that benevolence with all peoples.

However, it became an inescapable requirement that humanity conduct its life in accordance with God's will. For this purpose, God has provided statutes and commandments. If man will but observe them, he will find life therein and length of days, well-being and peace. But these commands are not arbitrary and capricious, designed to trap man into sin, make him stumble and fall in his humanness. Nor are they beyond the reach of human aspiration or capacity to perform them: "It is not in heaven . . . nor beyond the sea . . . but in thy mouth and in thy heart that thou mayest do it" (Deut. 30: 11–16; 19).

Similarly, the entire prophetic movement, from Amos on, assumes the capability and responsibility of men, and of Israelites in particular, to perform God's will.

Man, to be sure, is constantly tempted. But temptation, as symbolized by the biblical serpent, does not have its lair in man's heart, for he comes to Eve and Adam from without. "There is no notion that the original constitution of Adam underwent any change in consequence of the fall, so that he transmitted to his descendants a vitiated nature in which the appetites and passions necessarily prevail over reason and virtue, while the will to good is enfeebled or wholly impotent." (G. F. Moore, *Judaism*, Vol. I, p. 479). Thus·in the case of Cain, the first murderer, the sin which "coucheth at the door" of Cain's heart like a wild beast does not have its den within him, where Augustine finds it; but instead, Cain may indeed "rule over it."

Fully in line with the biblical view was the Rabbis':

"Should you say that the evil impulse is not in your power, I (God) have declared unto you in Scripture, 'Unto thee is its desire, but thou mayest rule over it,' " (Genesis *Rabbah*, xxii, 6).

That a people who traced their origins to pessimistic Babylonia should yet develop a fresh and confident outlook on life underscores the originality of the Jewish achievement. Abraham must have left Ur of the Chaldees in the period of its prosperity or only incipient decline in the 20th century, but definitely before its utter destruction by the Elamites about 1960 B.C.E. In any event, there was a complete mental and emotional dissociation from the homeland, so that Abraham and his followers were not affected by Ur's catastrophe or by the outlook of despair that accompanied and contributed to its collapse. But far more important, the Israelites underwent an unforgettable experience early in their history which shaped their outlook for all time—the liberation from bondage in Egypt.

No condition of man was more abject than that of servitude in antiquity. Slavery over generations, such as held the Israelites in Egypt, might have produced the fixation that they were victims of cosmic forces which had plotted their everlasting degradation. Disintegration of the group would have followed.

But there arose a Moses, the man who himself was free, even a princeling, yet who voluntarily cast in his lot with his brethren, identified his future with their plight and impelled them to freedom. Moses taught them that not he but God wrought the great deliverance. For the first time in history, the most abject and degraded class of man, the slave, who had no share in his master's religious cult, experienced God as just and compassionate, and felt himself to be the personal recipient of His beneficence. The descendants of those Israelites were never permitted to forget that experience of redemption by God as evidence of His justice and compassion and the fulfillment of a pledge to the Fathers. In this manner, Egyptian bondage was made to yield the very opposite of forlornness and disintegration. The redemption was so interpreted as to induce a sense of security and a feeling of belonging to one another. From this awareness of one another as the beneficiaries—equally—of divine justice and compassion, arose the awareness of other peoples as equally His beneficiaries, even though they might be the arch-enemies of Israel:

"I did, indeed, bring up Israel out of the Land of Egypt; but so also the Philistines from Caphtor and the Arameans from Kir" (Amos 9:7).

Thereby they caught a glimpse of the Source of the process which makes for the dignity and the humanization of man.

The remarkable biblical injunction, "Thou shalt love the Lord Thy God with all thy heart and with all thy soul and with all thy might," is evidence of only one fact, namely, that the author has experienced God's compassion and justice and is convinced that He loves man with all His might and main. His own love of God is a quick natural response. Similarly, a feeling of belonging in God's world and to one's fellow-man in a like-minded community could evoke kindly impulses and make the Jew responsive to the sympathetic feelings of his neighbors. The injunction of *Leviticus,* "Thou shalt love thy neighbor as thyself," tells us at once that the author is aware of kindly feelings within himself, as in his neighbor, inpulses which are *worthy* of love.

The alienated individual finds his own unfriendly drives mirrored in every act of his neighbor. How can he love him when he loathes himself for those very designs? The alienated individual is as little capable of love of God or fellowman as of himself. The person (or society) who feels himself to be the victim of implacable, arbitrary forces is likely to give measure for measure to God and to man.

In summary, there came to be embedded in the Jewish religious culture a conviction that God is merciful and just. In His compassion, He has provided for man's basic needs and has so endowed him that he may attain his own well-being through fulfillment of the divine will. God is just. He does not rule by caprice, but subjects Himself to the moral law. He requires that His creatures do no less. If they should sin, He metes out punishment. But man does not sin in consequence of a corrupt nature which seduces him to transgression. On the contrary, man's endowment is of divine origin and he possesses the capacity to perform God's will and enjoy the benefits thereof. Hence, even God's punishment, when meted out for sin, is roooted in His justice and mercy. And even now, penalty may still be avoided. Genuine contrition and repentance are man's key to a new start, to a re-direction of his capacities toward the end that God intended. Out of such fresh and original insights, sprang some of the most meaningful convictions of Judaism.

One of these convictions is that evil, especially social evil and injustice, is a negation of God's purpose, inasmuch as it opposes the welfare of man and society. Hence, it must be eradicated, "Thou shall cauterize the evil from out of the midst of thee."

One young person summed up for himself and several of his fellow-students the mood of our age in these words:

"There has always been corruption and dishonesty and there always will be. That is the nature of man. All you can hope to do is learn to beat the 'system' so that it doesn't corrupt you completely."

To which a fellow-student replied:

"The progress in medicine and the resulting longevity of our time, show that we can do something about social evil too. Science achieved its progress through the use of intelligence, a close analysis of the problem and a determined effort to find a solution. We can do the same with social evil."

In Jewish religious terms, we would say that it is possible for man to achieve a better world order by putting to use his God-given powers of mind, purpose and feeling. Judaism has refused to assent to any doctrine of the hopelessness of evil's removal, or the helplessness of man. Rather is man a collaborator in God's purpose, the *shuttaf hakadosh barukh hu,* when he strives after the eradication of evil.

Is the Jewish outlook more "true" than others? Yes, indeed, if love is better than hatred, reciprocal trust preferable to mutual destruction.

All of human existence is a pilgrimage toward a better world. Through the partnership and inter-dependence of God and man, the good and right can triumph in the end, and God's law will come to be writ on every man's heart while "the earth will be full of the knowledge of the Lord as the waters cover the sea."

BIBLIOGRAPHY

For a general history of modern Judaism see the following: Jacob Katz, *Exclusiveness and Toleration: Studies in Jewish-Gentile Relations in Modern Times* [Down to the eighteenth century] (New York: 1961). Howard L. Sachar, *The Course of Modern Jewish History* (Cleveland: 1958). Though it antedates 1500, for early Jewish history see Salo W. Baron, *Social and Religious History of the Jews* (2nd ed., rev. and enl. 8 vols. and index; New York: 1959–60). Other readings having to do with the "age of anxiety" are: Franklin L. Baumer, "Twentieth-Century Version of the Apocalypse," *Journal of World History,* I (1954), 623–640. Christopher Dawson, *The Movement of World Revolution* (New York: 1959). Reinhold Niebuhr, *Nature and Destiny of Man* (New York: 1953). José Ortega y Gasset,

Man and Crisis (New York: 1958). Morton White (ed.), *The Age of Analysis* [Readings in twentieth-century philosophy] (New York: 1955). [The Editor.]

REFLECTIONS ON RELIGION AND MODERN INDIVIDUALISM *

Herbert Butterfield

In the search for those unique elements that have given western civilization its intellectual liveliness and variety during the past five hundred years, one of the most significant and oft-cited characteristics is its stress upon the individual personality and self-development. Precisely how and why this peculiar emphasis on individualism came to be a part of the western tradition has long been the subject of speculation. In explanation, Professor Herbert Butterfield suggests that here, as in so many other things, the western religious tradition made an important contribution. Moreover, he adds that many of the assumptions of our own secular age are deeply rooted in the religious values of preceding periods of history without our really being aware of it. Here, then, is an excellent summation of certain significant aspects of western religious history from the Reformation to the present day.

One of the features of our modern history is a sort of heightening of the notion of individual responsibility, and the dissemination of this amongst wider sections of the population. It gives Western man the appearance of being adult and self-standing; and I am not sure that it is quite paralleled in the other civilizations of the globe. The individual, fighting for "freedom of conscience," is asserting (perhaps against authority and custom) his responsibility for his own religion. Before the Reformation, before there was the stimulus of doctrinal conflict, the laymen in various regions seem to have begun to take more of a hand in the life of the Church. But in the subsequent controversies considerable numbers of people were involved (through their religion) in wider national issues, and the great feature of the

---

* Reprinted with the permission of the author and the editors of the *Journal of the History of Ideas* (XXII, 1961, 33–46, with omissions).

West is the growing sense of responsibility for public affairs. What is remarkable today is the way in which an undergraduate or an artisan is liable to feel a responsibility when he thinks of the nuclear weapon, the treatment of African natives, or the future of the food-problem in India. If earlier ages had a parallel to this feeling of responsibility and this oecumenical solicitude, it was perhaps in the spirit which moved those missionaries who travelled to the ends of the earth for the saving of souls. A Russian aristocrat, who had returned to her homeland some time after the Revolution, was quoted to me as having reported that, though the atrocities had been great, she had been surprised to find the peasants (whom in the old days they had regarded as rather like cows) straightening their backs and holding up their heads. Whether this was true or not, it points to a recognizable aspect of our modern development—a Western "progress" that had a "moral" significance.

In the early modern centuries the movement is part of our religious history. It tends to be hostile to whatever may be the presiding Church; and it works to the undoing of the state as a "religious society."

At first it seemed that the Reformation might result in the hardening of the notion of a "Christian Commonwealth." Martin Luther did not intend its relaxation; he was concerned rather to establish right religion in the world. The Reformation, especially since it led to the principle of *cujus regio ejus religio,* encouraged Caesaropapism on the scale of the nation-state. Authority was tightened, or was felt as more oppressive; and now it was a case of a tyranny more close at hand. We ought to be surprised at the firmness of those dissident consciences which checked the rise of this imposing power. Yet the dissidents themselves were often seeking to establish their own equally authoritarian system.

We today find it curious that men who insisted on the voice of conscience within themselves, and were willing enough to suffer for their own consciences, were so unable to see the case for the other man's conscience. In a way, the interior nature of religion—and the internal sanction for it—were genuinely recognized; but, while faith was so militant and authoritarian, it could not be admitted that more than one choice was really open to the individual. Since religion was an absolute, and there could be only one absolute, the religious dissident could not be regarded as really representing a case of conscience at all. It would seem that, from a mundane point of view, a religion claiming to be supernatural can be a dangerous thing for the world, unless it has as its over-ruling principle the kind of "charity" which presses towards imaginative understanding.

The modern centuries achieved a reconciliation between the absolutism of revealed religion and the relativity which the recognition of the individual conscience seemed to entail. The transition appears to be an easy one in retrospect, for we today are not imprisoned in dreams of a "Christian society," or in notions of celestial and diabolical systems, semi-materialist in character. We can take our start from a clearer recognition of the interior and voluntarist nature of religion. In the XVIIth century the process required a higher exercise of sympathetic understanding, and I wonder whether I am right in feeling that in the XVIIth century the principle of "charity" was gaining ground, or developing in a more imaginative way. I remember seeing the principle adduced in Cromwellian England in order to persuade people to put themselves in the other man's place, and to realize that the other man was following his conscience too. It was more easy for a time to adopt this attitude towards other kinds of Protestants than towards Roman Catholics. The duty of dealing with others in the way in which one would want them to deal with oneself is seen by Thomas Hobbes as the fundamental law of nature, the thing that was really self-evident.

Concerning the rôle of religion in the history of liberty we can say that the claim for "freedom of conscience" arose out of Christianity, and that the dream of a "Christian society" was first shattered by pious men. These did not intend freedom for the people who differed from them, however; and, far from meaning to break "the Christian Commonwealth," they were often conducting a crusade for the purpose of re-shaping it to their heart's desire. It was the situation—the rise of competing versions of Christianity, and the failure of any one of these to drive out the rest—which impelled the world to ideas of religious liberty far removed from the original intention. Some may feel that the very pressures of the predicament compelled Christianity, in its organized form, to revert to its original nature, or to become more faithful to its essential principles. Before the end of the story, a religious ideal of "freedom of conscience" had distinctly emerged; and this was not without significance. But the process was too slow, and it looks as if the tragedy worked itself out to the bitter end, toleration being imposed to a great degree by mundane interests, almost as a gift from the World to the Church. It must have owed much to war-weariness, the coming of religious indifference, the rise of a rationalism associated with the scientific movement, and the

development of a relativist attitude, partly encouraged by the coexistence of multiple forms of Christianity, partly produced by the
dawning realization that, in global history, Christianity looked like a
regional affair. Historical conjunctures, political calculations, economic motives, even at moments the desperate state of governmental
finances, induced kings now to make compromises in the wars of religion, now to abandon the ideal of uniformity in their own lands.
At times the case against continued persecution seems to have been
presented as the protest of a terrestrial morality against a morality
supposed to be supra-terrestrial. One would think that religious
liberty might have been achieved in Europe in ways less painful,
ways perhaps less harmful to the cause of religion itself. Churchmen,
however, had understandably gone on clinging to the beautiful dream
of the uniform "religious society," existing to the glory of God. There
are mixtures of the spiritual and the mundane that seem like poetry
at first, but then become more sinister than mere self-regarding politics, and have to be rectified, if necessary, by some clean worldly-
mindedness.

The existence of religious dissent within the Church-State systems
of the post-Reformation period had important effects on the wider history of freedom. It was the nonconformists who were in the best position for continuing the conflict which the spiritual authority had waged
against the temporal in the Middle Ages. Since they were unable to
adduce either the *fiat* of the king or the verdict of society in their
support, they had to place entire reliance on a higher authority outside
the state. In relation to the whole existing order, they were fixed at an
angle of permanent hostility, a body absolutely predisposed for criticism, the precursors of the whole system of a standing opposition within
the state. They not only brought to the criticism of the existing order
criteria from entirely outside that order, but in one sense they tran-
scended the rôle which the medieval church had fulfilled in relation to
the secular authorities. They had recently emerged from what might be
called "insurrectionary" forms of Christianity, ready with radical criticisms of the religious society as it had hitherto existed, and more eager
than official Christianity to refer everything back to first principles or
scriptural teaching. The compound nature of the politico-ecclesiastical
systems then existing, and their own grievances against the government
of the day, made it almost inevitable that religious dissidents should
become the apostles of political and social revolution or reform.

In the early modern centuries the egalitarian principle reappears—
and now, perhaps, to greater effect than before—still basing itself on the

idea of the equality of all men in the sight of God. There are fallacies in the argument, but where the spiritual and the mundane are so entangled—where society is supposed to be a "Christian society"—it must have seemed natural to claim rights for the lowliest classes on the ground that Christ had made all men free. Already in the XVIth century, religious radicalism was associated with communistic experiments, and here the practices of the early Church had an understandable influence. Apart from the political and social speculations in Cromwellian England, John Bellers, before the end of the XVIIth century, was producing the socialistic design which influenced Robert Owen.

Nonconformity performed its famous function as a result of the predicament in which it stood. Men who held the same doctrinal principles were soon working to a different purpose when they had captured the government and achieved settled authority over the body politic. Nor could it be said that nonconformity performs its historic function at the present day, when it is no longer set at an angle of predisposed hostility. Perhaps it tends rather to be part of the Establishment, seeing the preservation of the existing régime as essential to religion itself. It would almost be true to say that the rôle of standing opposition and the function of radical criticism which had belonged to nonconformity in England, passed (particularly in France) to what might be called the "lapsed Christians," who had a good deal of the same outlook, so far as mundane affairs were concerned, but separated it entirely from religious dogma. Some of them claimed to be better followers of Christ than the Christians, because they put the principle of charity before rites and ceremonies; and it seemed that their breach with the Church enabled them to emancipate themselves from conventionalities and work more freely for objects which the Churches themselves count as good at the present day. At a later stage again, there were still more militant enemies of religion who stood out in the same way as the boldest and most radical critics of the existing order. It sometimes happened that the criticisms which these people had to make were a repetition or extension of ones which religious dissidents had been the first to put forward. Sometimes the reforms which had been first demanded by religious minorities were put into execution through the efforts of non-Christians, and against the bitter resistance of churchmen. Sometimes the enemies of religion have brought out criticisms of society which one is surprised that Christians themselves had not been the first to make. In all this there may be a criticism of historical Christianity, so far as concerns its relations with society, at least in modern times.

It seems clear, however, that in the XVIth and XVIIth centuries it would have been dangerous—dangerous even to liberty and individualism—if the religious dissidents had been left in command of the field. Where they secured local predominance for a moment the sects produced their own tyranny and then generally provoked a reaction. The churches which worked rather in the defense of the existing régime would seem therefore to have had their own important function to perform; and the radicalism of the religious dissidents perhaps helps to explain the intensified conservatism of the other party.

When a civilization, which has been developing for a thousand years under a presiding religion, breaks away from such tutelage, it becomes interesting to know how far anything of that religion lingers on in modes of thought, unconscious assumptions, and the basic structure of the human outlook. If a number of religious civilizations have been through this process independently, the result may be superficially the same in each case, but a closer examination may show that profounder divergencies exist. In each case, the character of the prevailing religion may have influenced mental habits and human attitudes, or branded its patterns on the basic material of the culture that has undergone the secularization. I remember hearing a citizen of Pakistan described as a secular liberal, and being told that his mind had been considerably "westernized"; yet I gather that, on the last analysis, his thought still revealed subtle preconceptions or inclinations only to be explained through Mohammedan legal ideas that go back for many centuries.

A general secularization of thought is visible in Western Europe from about 1700, and, in a very real sense, from about that time, the Church loses its former leadership in society. Many of the mundane values of the previous generations still persisted, however, though separated from Christian dogma; and, indeed, the influence of religion over the masses and over much of the intelligentsia itself remains remarkable until almost the present century. Mazzini said that the French Revolution did not herald a new age (for Italy herself was about to do that) but merely wound up the old one, the era of Christianity, the era of Individualism. In the XVIIIth century, as religion declined, the secular writers seemed to talk more than ever of "conscience" and the "rights of conscience," taking over from their religious predecessors an idea eminently capable of laicization. The political radicals in England picked up not only the ideals but also the techniques and the machinery of the nonconformist; and, for example, the new types of radical club, which terrified Pitt and the aristocracy in 1792, took over the organization and the penny-a-week payments of the Methodist "class-meeting," with occasionally a prayer and a democratic hymn, as well as readings from Tom Paine instead of the Bible. It would be difficult to measure to what a degree there lurks (below the level of our conscious intellectual systems) a residue of assumptions about life on the earth, or the dim shape of a view about the nature of man, which go back to religious ages more remote.

Just as American humor differs from English humor (and I imagine that the differences would be delicate matters to explain) it would seem that American notions of liberty may differ subtly from British notions, diverging somewhat, for example, in respect of freedom of the press. It is possible to imagine intellectual contexts in which Acton's principle of "freedom of conscience" would seem either implausible or unimportant or devoid of any foothold for effective defense. An idea which seems as clear and clean as that of liberty may rest on unseen foundations—Acton thought, for example, that liberty was impossible except amongst peoples who were conscious of living under an invisible system of over-ruling law. Events in the XXth century suggest that a particular kind of respect for personality, which has become second nature to us, must not be merely taken for granted, as though it would exist amongst people who were traditionless. It must be regarded as the product of a complicated process. The historian is wrong if he tries to trace things back to a single cause, which is the source of all the other causes. Modern individualism perhaps requires for its explanation nothing less than the narrative of all our preceding history.

It is difficult to see how individualism could have developed as it did, or how Western civilization could have become so dynamic, without the remarkable economic expansion of Western Europe. When we see how the spirit of enterprise could spread from industry and commerce to other fields, or how exhilarating the life of cities could become, we might feel that economic progress is not merely the condition but the actual cause of modern individualism. The main seats of the Renaissance in Italy, South Germany, and the Netherlands were on the old line of Eastern trade, and in city-states that had flourished on industry and commerce. Holland and England played a leading part in the history of liberty at a time when they, in turn, had come into the path of economic advance.

All the same, it is not so clear, now, as once it seemed to be, that economic opportunity and economic development must necessarily bring freer play for the individual (rather than more elaborate slave-systems or tyrannical trading kings) unless there is a prior bias towards individualism in the form of the existing order. It is possible that tendencies to individualism were partly the cause and not merely the result of the dynamic character of the European economy in later medieval and early modern times. I am not sure that absolutely inescapable economic necessities (independent of any constricting effects of Catholicism) provide us with the complete and sufficient explanation of the decline of Spain, after the glories of its Golden Age.

If by "individualism" we mean vigorous and luxuriant life, and the sheer multiplicity of human types, it would seem that nature can be prodigal in personalities, eccentric figures and varieties of style, even where there is tyrannical government—even, indeed, in a Dickensian slum. (At the same time the XVIIIth century, even where it made almost a religion of "individualism," can surprise us by its uniformities and conventionalities in matters of taste.) But if by 'individualism" we have in mind the autonomy of men who are determined to decide the main purpose of their lives and feel a similar responsibility for public affairs (so that they move to a greater command of their destiny, and may decide to have democratic government even if they believe it militarily less efficient)—here is something which depends on the existence and transmission of a complicated body of inherited assumptions and ideas.

BIBLIOGRAPHY

Herbert Butterfield, *Christianity and History* (New York: 1950); *Christianity and European History* (Oxford: 1951). Christopher Dawson, *Understanding Europe* (New York, 1952). Carleton J. H. Hayes, *Christianity and Western Civilization* (Stanford, Calif.: 1954). Reinhold Niebuhr, *Faith in History* (New York, 1949). John H. Randall, Jr., *The Role of Knowledge in Western Religion* (Boston: 1958). Arnold Toynbee, *An Historian's Approach to Religion* (Oxford: 1956). Basil Willey, *Christianity Past and Present* (Cambridge, Eng.: 1952). [The Editor.]

PB 2295-D